# THE VIOLENT HOME
## A Study of Physical Aggression
## Between Husbands and Wives

**Volume 13, Sage Library of Social Research**

# SAGE LIBRARY OF SOCIAL RESEARCH

1. David Caplovitz:
   The Merchants of Harlem
2. James N. Rosenau:
   International Studies and the Social
   Sciences
3. Douglas E. Ashford:
   Ideology and Participation
4. Patrick J. McGowan and
   Howard B. Shapiro:
   The Comparative Study of Foreign
   Policy
5. George A. Male:
   The Struggle for Power
6. Raymond Tanter:
   Modelling and Managing
   International Conflicts
7. Anthony James Catanese:
   Planners and Local Politics
8. James Russell Prescott:
   Economic Aspects of Public Housing
9. F. Parkinson:
   Latin America, the Cold War, and the
   World Powers, 1945-1973
10. Robert G. Smith:
    Ad Hoc Governments
11. Ronald Gallimore, Joan Whitehorn
    Boggs, and Cathie Jordan:
    Culture, Behavior and Education
12. Howard W. Hallman:
    Neighborhood Government in a
    Metropolitan Setting
13. Richard J. Gelles:
    The Violent Home
14. Jerry L. Weaver:
    Conflict and Control in Health Care
    Administration
15. Gebhard Ludwig Schweigler:
    National Consciousness in Divided
    Germany
16. James T. Carey:
    Sociology and Public Affairs
17. Edward W. Lehman:
    Coordinating Health Care
18. Charles G. Bell and Charles M. Price:
    The First Term
19. Clayton P. Alderfer and
    L. Dave Brown:
    Learning from Changing
20. L. Edward Wells and Gerald Marwell:
    Self-Esteem
21. Robert S. Robins:
    Political Institutionalization and the
    Integration of Elites
22. William R. Schonfeld:
    Obedience and Revolt
23. William C. McCready and
    Andrew M. Greeley:
    The Ultimate Values of the American
    Population
24. F. Ivan Nye:
    Role Structure and Analysis of the
    Family
25. Paul Wehr and Michael Washburn:
    Peace and World Order Systems
26. Patricia R. Stewart:
    Children in Distress
27. Juergen Dedring:
    Recent Advances in Peace and
    Conflict Research
28. Moshe M. Czudnowski:
    Comparing Political Behavior
29. Jack D. Douglas:
    Investigative Social Research
30. Michael Stohl:
    War and Domestic Political Violence
31. Nancy E. Williamson:
    Sons or Daughters
32. Werner Levi:
    Law and Politics in the International
    Society
33. David L. Altheide:
    Creating Reality
34. Allan Lerner:
    The Politics of Decision-Making
35. Philip E. Converse:
    The Dynamics of Party Support
36. Charles L. Newman and
    Barbara R. Price:
    Jails and Drug Treatment
37. Clarence L. Abercrombie III:
    The Military Chaplain
38. Mark Gottdiener:
    Planned Sprawl
39. Robert L. Lineberry:
    Equality and Urban Policy
40. Patrick M. Morgan:
    Deterrence
41. Vladimir A. Lefebvre:
    The Structure of Awareness
42. Andrea Fontana:
    The Last Frontier
43. Robert V. Kemper:
    Migration and Adaptation
44. David Caplovitz and Fred Sherrow:
    The Religious Drop-Outs
45. Stuart S. Nagel and Marian Neef:
    The Legal Process: Modeling the
    System
46. Rue Bucher and Joan G. Stelling:
    Becoming Professional
47. Paul Hiniker:
    Revolutionary Ideology and Chinese
    Reality
48. Simon N. Herman:
    Jewish Identity
49. Alan Marsh:
    Protest and Political Consciousness
50. Ralph LaRossa:
    Conflict and Power in Marriage
51. Bengt Abrahamsson:
    Bureaucracy or Participation
52. F. Parkinson:
    The Philosophy of International
    Relations
53. Lars Lerup:
    Building the Unfinished
54. Arthur L. Smith, Jr.:
    Churchill's German Army
55. Carol Corden:
    Planned Cities
56. Howard W. Hallman:
    Small and Large Together
57. James A. Inciardi, Alan A. Block, and
    Lyle A. Hallowell:
    Historical Approaches to Crime
58. Sar A. Levitan and
    Karen Cleary Alderman:
    Warriors at Work
59. Louis A. Zurcher, Jr.:
    The Mutable Self
60. Henry Teune and Zdravko Mlinar:
    The Developmental Logic of Social
    Systems
61. G. David Garson:
    Group Theories of Politics
62. Linda Medcalf:
    Law and Identity
63. James N. Danziger:
    Making Budgets
64. Joseph Damrell:
    Search for Identity
65. Ezra Stotland et al.:
    Empathy, Fantasy and Helping
66. Jonathan David Aronson:
    Money and Power

# The Violent Home

A Study of Physical Aggression
Between Husbands and Wives

## Richard J. Gelles

Volume 13
SAGE LIBRARY OF
SOCIAL RESEARCH

Published in Cooperation with the
National Council on Family Relations

 **SAGE PUBLICATIONS**    Beverly Hills    London

*For information address:*

**SAGE** PUBLICATIONS, INC.
275 South Beverly Drive
Beverly Hills, California 90212

**SAGE** PUBLICATIONS LTD
28 Banner Street
London EC1Y 8QE, England

Printed in the United States of America   0-8039-0449-5(P)

International Standard Book Number 0-8039-0381-2(C)

Library of Congress Catalog Card No.  73-94288

THIRD PRINTING

*To my wife Judy and my father Sidney S. Gelles*

# CONTENTS

*Chapter*                                                                          *Page*

   Acknowledgments                                                            11

   Foreword by Murray A. Straus                                               13

1. A Study of Conjugal Violence                                                    19

2. Incidence, Methods, and Meanings of Intrafamily Violence                        47

3. No Place to Go: The Violent Situation                                           93

4. The Rose Garden: Social and Family Structure                                   119

5. "It Takes Two": The Roles of Victim and Offender                               155

6. Basic Training for Violence                                                     169

7. A Social Structure of Violence                                                  183

   References                                                                 195

   Appendix A                                                                 205

   Appendix B                                                                 217

   Author Index                                                               223

   Subject Index                                                              225

   About the Author                                                           231

# LIST OF TABLES AND FIGURES

**TABLES**

1. Percent of Total Conjugal Violence by Source of Respondent — 49
2. Percent of Husband to Wife and Wife to Husband Violence by Source of Respondent — 51
3. Percent of Husbands and Wives Who *Ever Used* Violence on Each Other by Method of Violence — 53
4. Percent of Total Parental Violence by Source of Respondent — 54
5. Percent of Father and Mother to Child Violence by Source of Respondent — 56
6. Percent of Mothers and Fathers Who *Ever Used* Violence on Their Children by Method of Violence — 57
7. Spatial Locations of Conjugal Violence Mentioned by Respondents — 95
8. Time of Day of Conjugal Violence Mentioned by Respondents — 100
9. Day of the Week of Conjugal Violence Mentioned by Respondents — 104
10. Percent of Conjugal Violence by Sex and Age — 122
11. Percent of Conjugal Violence by Education — 122
12. Percent of Frequent Conjugal Violence by Education — 123
13. Percent of Conjugal Violence by Occupational Status — 124
14. Percent of Frequent Conjugal Violence by Occupational Status — 125
15. Percent of Conjugal Violence by Family Income — 126

16. Percent of Frequent Conjugal Violence by Family Income   126
17. Percent of Conjugal Violence by Sex and Religion   127
18. Comparison of Families with Conjugal Violence to Neighbors with *No* Conjugal Violence   131
19. Conjugal Violence by Educational Difference Between Spouses   138
20. Conjugal Violence by Difference in Occupational Status Between Spouses   138
21. Conjugal Violence by Difference in Age Between Spouses   138
22. Conjugal Violence by Number of Children   149
23. Conjugal Violence by Religious Difference   151
24. Percent of Respondents Who Physically Fought With Spouse by Respondent's Observation of Conjugal Violence in Family of Orientation   173
25. Percent of Respondents Who Physically Fought with Spouse by Parental Violence Toward Respondent as Child   174
26. Marital Status of Respondents by Source of Respondent   205
27. Length of Respondent's Marriage by Source of Respondent   206
28. Number of Children by Source of Respondent   207
29. Education by Sex and Source of Respondent   208
30. Occupation of Husbands   209
31. Occupational Status by Sex and Source of Respondent   210
32. Occupation of Wives   210
33. Total Family Income by Source of Respondent   211
34. Religion by Sex and Source of Respondent   212
35. Age by Sex and Source of Respondent   213

## FIGURES

1. A Typology of Family Violence   86
2. A Model of Intrafamily Violence   186

# ACKNOWLEDGMENTS

This project was born in work with Murray A. Straus. He convinced me during a number of conversations that research on violence between spouses would contribute to a wide gap in our knowledge of the family. I owe a great debt to Murray for his guidance, patience, and encouragement during the design and conduct of this study. His scholarly wisdom, his suggestions, and most of all, his enthusiasm were major contributions to this monograph.

Stuart Palmer, Pauline Soukaris, Stephen Weber, Daniel Williams, and Cecilia Sudia all contributed greatly to this research through their suggestions, thoughtful reading, and criticisms of parts of this work.

My professor, advisor, and friend Howard Shapiro cannot be thanked enough for his suggestions and help during this study and for the countless hours of professional and personal support.

The actual research would not have been possible without the cooperation and assistance of Child and Family Services of New Hampshire and the Portsmouth Police Department. I would like to thank Albert Chicoine, Alice White, Mary Copithorne, and the staff of Child and Family Services of New Hampshire for their time and effort on behalf of this project. In addition, Marshall Stanley Remick and Officer W. Richard Ferguson were of great assistance in the research.

Forty interviews were conducted by Susan Getman. She was an outstanding interviewer who contributed many perceptive ideas to the final interview schedule. Moreover, she was a pleasure to work with.

Two young ladies who had the most difficult job were Eileen Soule and Lori Tomsic. They spent many long hours hunched over typewriter and tape recorder transcribing the interviews. To them I owe a special thanks for their devoted service.

I am truly indebted to Trixie McLain and Betty Jones who painstakingly typed and retyped portions of the manuscript.

Funding for this study came from NIMH grants MH 15521-04, MH 13050-01, and MH 24002-01.

Last is my acknowledgment to my wife, Judy. Unlike other wives who are mentioned at this point, she neither sweated long hours coding interviews, nor did she faithfully fill the chore of typing the manuscript. But she, more than anyone, provided the inspiration and encouragement for the work required to complete this study. She made it worth all the effort.

## THE RESPONDENTS

There is one group of individuals without whose help the research truly could not have taken place—the 80 respondents who generously gave up time from their day to talk to total strangers about intimate and personal parts of their lives. In order to protect the rights and anonimity of these people, certain changes have been made in their statements. Occupations, names, number of children, and other possibly identifying factors have been slightly altered to preserve their privacy. To these 80 people, I am truly and deeply indebted.

# FOREWORD

"Selective inattention" is a useful way of characterizing research on violence in the family, especially husband-wife violence. It is true that social workers and psychiatrists have examined the issue in studies of "battered wives." But it is implicit in these clinical studies that husband-wife violence is seen as a relatively rare type of behavior traceable to individual pathology. Until very recently, sociologists and psychologists have done even less: they have almost completely ignored husband-wife violence.

The relegation of husband-wife violence to a form of individual pathology by social workers and psychiatrists, and the ignoring of it by sociologists and psychologists, can be traced to a number of factors. One of these seems to be the social definition of the family as nonviolent. This causes a perceptual·blackout of the family violence going on daily all around us in "normal" families. In a similar way the theoretical stance which has dominated American sociology—that of functionalist, consensus, and integration theory—has also desensitized or diverted attention away from family conflict in general, and conflict which uses physical force in particular. Finally, and perhaps most important of all, Gelles' study suggests that these socially shared definitions of the family as nonviolent seem to lead husbands and wives to define and construct instances in which physical force is used as something other than "violence." Therefore, violence in the family has not emerged as a social problem because no sizable or influential group in the population has defined it as a problem.

The recent emergence of family violence as a focus of research must be examined in terms of the same cultural and social forces which caused its former neglect. First, the public and social scientists have been sensitized to violence because of such events as the slaughter in Vietnam, political assassinations, rising homicide and assault rates, and violent social and political protest.

Second, the reemergence of the women's movement seems likely to have played a part. It is women who are the more frequent victims of husband-wife violence and fewer women will now tolerate this. One indication is the explosive growth of shelter homes for "battered wives." Five have been set up in just the few months I have been in England to meet a problem which has been present for ages. Moreover, at least in England, the battered-wife shelters are far more than shelters. They are also political entities and strong points from which salvos are regularly issued against contemporary family patterns and sexual inequality. Even more fundamental is the fact that the actual or implicit threat of physical coercion is one of the many factors underlying male dominance in the family. Thus, slaps and threats which formerly were defined as nonviolent are defined as "violence"; that is, as illegitimate use of force.

Finally, the dominance of the consensus model of society has been under increasing challenge by conflict and social action models of society. In the consensus model, society is viewed as a system of relatively harmonious parts which is disrupted from time to time by conflict. In the conflict model, society is viewed as a system whose *normal* state is one of conflict between its parts. But the importance of the conflict perspective goes far beyond merely asserting that conflict is a ubiquitous part of social interaction. The more important difference lies in the view that conflict is essential if groups are not to stagnate and if different individuals and groups are to secure justice.

The three factors just mentioned (public sensitization to recent violent events, the women's movement, and the decline of the consensus paradigm of society) are by no means a sufficient accounting for the recent emergence of studies of intrafamily violence. Rather, they illustrate how the same set of social forces, which in one era produce selective inattention, in another time period "create" a social problem out of behavior which is in no way different than that which previously existed.

The emergence of a new social problem, however, is not the same as the emergence of valid research on that problem. The research up to now has approached family violence tangentially. The reason for this is to be found in the focus on wife-beating as a relatively infrequent type of individual pathology and, as Gelles notes, because husband-wife violence has been a taboo topic. Thus it was only felt worthwhile or even possible to study groups such as those seeking psychiatric or social assistance, or among those in a situation of already acknowledged marital conflict such as divorce petitioners. The study reported in this book marks a major step in the development of research on family violence because Gelles was able to study not only those in such special circumstances, but also an equal number of families who had no contact with agencies of social service or control. Gelles' comparison group are the next door neighbors of his agency and "police" families. Obviously, this is not a random sample of families. But it is the closest yet available to the study of violence in a representative sample of families. His findings therefore provide the best available data on the frequency of husband-wife violence, and they will be eyeopeners for some. Even so, my own estimate is that for various reasons the frequency of husband-wife violence is actually greater than was found for this sample.

The main contribution of this study, however, is not the figures on how often husbands and wives attack each other—important as that is. Rather it is the rich detail concerning the social meaning of violent acts as felt by the participants;

the locus of these events in time and space; the way the family serves as a training ground for violent behavior; and above all, the demonstration that violence is related to position in the family in the social structure and to the role structure of individual families.

All of these findings point to the limitations of the "individual pathology" approach to family violence which has dominated the field up to now. Gelles' ground-breaking empirical study, together with the social structural theory of violence with which he concludes, suggests that individual pathology is but a minor element. Few, if any, of the people he studied can be considered as suffering from any gross abnormality. Rather, the occurrence of physical violence in these families seems to reflect standard features of American society and patterns of family organization which can be found everywhere in American society.

This is not to say the Gelles' findings are conclusive or his theory definitive; both are put forward tentatively. Thus, for those whose interest in family violence is centered on research and theory, his work points the way to an array of needed studies. But granting the tentative nature of the findings and the theory, in my judgment they nonetheless provide a more comprehensive factual and theoretical basis for understanding family violence than has heretofore been available. Thus, for those whose interest in family violence is centered on ameliorating a social problem, his work points the way to social actions which truly will deal with the roots of the problem in the structure of society. In this context, assisting individual families experiencing violence is certainly necessary, but it is less fundamental than efforts to overcome such basic structural causes as the cultural heritage of violence transmitted by word and by example in millions of American families, the frustrations imposed on both men and women by the sexist organization of family and society, the social isolation from a community of kin and neighbors experienced by so many families in modern industrial societies, and the frustrations created by the discrepancy between the economic aspirations so effectively inculcated and the inability of our society (and probably any society) to fulfill these aspirations for everyone.

Murray A. Straus
*University of York*
*York, England*
*May 1974*

# Chapter 1

# A STUDY OF CONJUGAL VIOLENCE

A 24-year-old South End woman and her one-year-old son were shot to death in their apartment building at 620 Tremont St.

Both bodies were reportedly found in the hallway of the apartment building.

The woman's husband . . . is being sought for questioning, police said.

Johnny Lindquist, unconscious since July 28 from a beating he received after being taken from a foster home and returned to his natural parents, died yesterday. He was 7 years old.

Standing in sharp contrast to the picture of the American family as the source of love, sympathy, understanding, and unlimited support is the realization that the family is also the source of assaults, violence, and homicide. The veneer of the family as a harmonious, gentle, and supportive institution is cracking from increasing evidence (such as the two newsclippings above from the *Boston Globe,* September 1, 1972, p. 38) that the family is also the scene of varying degrees of violent acts, ranging from the punishment of children to slapping, hitting, throwing objects, and sometimes a homicidal assault by one member of the family on another.

Perhaps it is the semisacred nature of the family in society that leads to the denial or the avoidance of considering violence between family members (Steinmetz and Straus, 1974). Or, perhaps research has not been conducted on violence between family members because researchers are reluctant to engage in research where they actually have to ask "When did you stop beating your wife?" While there has been some attention paid to the more public and serious cases of family violence, such as murder or child abuse, the day-to-day patterned and recurrent use of physical violence in the family suffers from a lack of research. This is evident in John O'Brien's finding that in the entire *Index* of the *Journal of Marriage and the Family* from its inception in 1939 through 1969 there is not one article that contains the word "violence" in the title (1971: 691). There is little to no research on the types, incidence, or causes of violent attacks between family members except where it results in death or a reportable injury to a child.

It is this aspect of family life—the use of physical violence by one family member on another—that will be examined. This work is concerned with violence in so far as it means a family member pushing, slapping, punching, kicking, knifing, shooting, or throwing an object at another family member. Examination of family violence here will focus primarily on violent attacks between husband and wife, because this is the area where the greatest lack of research exists. The use of physical force by a parent on a child has had a more extensive amount of work carried out on outright abuse (see U.S. Department of Health, Education and Welfare, *Bibliography on the Battered Child,* 1969) and parental aggression towards children as punishment (see, for example, Eron, Walder, and Lefkowitz, 1971; Sears, Maccoby, and Levin, 1957). Some illustrative material on parent-child violence is also presented, but the emphasis of the research will be on violence between husband and wife.

## THE TIP OF THE ICEBERG

There is some empirical evidence on violence between family members that indicates that violence in the family is a significant phenomenon in family life. Much of the available data on violence in the family examine violence where there is a victim and requires a response from agents of social control (police, coroner, legal system) or where the victim of the violence is a child. This section reviews the available data on family violence and proposes that these may only be the "tip of the iceberg" of family violence. Beneath this tip may be an even more extensive amount of day-to-day, nonlethal violent behavior.

### Homicide in the Family

The data on criminal homicides indicate that home strife contributes a major proportion of the number of murders committed in the United States. In Atlanta, domestic quarrels were a factor in 31% of the 255 homicides in 1972 (*Boston Globe,* 1973: 12). In Detroit, labeled the "deadliest city" because its homicide rate in 1972 was the highest of any American city with a population over 1 million (*Newsweek,* 1973a: 20), four out of five murders involved people who knew each other—friends, neighbors, and relatives (*Newsweek,* 1973a: 21). Of these, a large portion were between family members. The FBI reports that in 1969 homicides within the family accounted for one-fourth of all murders and more than one-half of these were spouse killings (Truninger, 1971: 259). Additional data are provided by Palmer (1972: 40), who found that in 1966 29% of all murders occurred between offender and victim who were members of the same family, and Wolfgang's study of criminal homicide in Philadelphia, which found that also in 24.7% of all criminal homicides occurring from 1948-1952 victim and offender were members of the same family (1958: 207). Wolfgang breaks down his data to reveal that of the 136 victims who had familial relations with their slayers, 100 were husbands or wives, 9 sons, 8 daughters, 3 mothers, 3 brothers, 2 fathers, 1 sister, and 10 others (1958: 207). Thus, the Wolfgang data reveal that the predominant mode of familial homicide is spousal, while filicide (or, a parent killing a child) is next.

## Assault

Aggravated assault, or an attack by an individual on another with the intention of inflicting bodily harm, sometimes falls within the same category of behavior as criminal homicide, where the difference between assault and homicide may be the speed of the ambulance or a chance factor (Pittman and Handy, 1964; Pokorny, 1965). Pittman and Handy's study of aggravated assault in St. Louis finds the wife or husband victim in 11% of aggravated assaults (1964: 467). Pittman and Handy found that in acts of homicide, a wife attacked her husband more than a husband attacked his wife, while the reverse was true in aggravated assaults (1964: 470). Overall, in both homicide and assault women are more likely to aggress against someone with whom they have an intimate relationship (Pittman and Handy, 1964: 468).

Pittman and Handy's (1964) study and Pokorny's research (1965) demonstrate the similarity of patterns of assault with patterns of homicide. Given this similarity and Wolfgang's data that victim and offender were members of the same family in almost one-fourth of criminal homicides, we can posit that familial assaults constitute a significant portion (perhaps 20 to 25%) of aggravated assaults.

## Child Abuse

The data on another form of family violence—the physical abuse of children by their parents—are much more variable. Gil (1971: 639) estimates that 6,000 children a year are beaten and battered by their parents. Helfer and Kempe (1968) estimate the range at tens of thousands. *Parade*

(1972: 10) cites a figure of 60,000 cases of child abuse a year that are reported (1972) while the *Denver Post* estimates 25,000 cases per year (Stoenner, 1972: 53). New York had 7,000 cases of child beating reported in 1971 (*Newsweek*, 1972: 66) while in Massachusetts 7,290 children were abused or neglected in 1972 (Liebowitz, 1972: 5-10). A recent reanalysis of Gil's data by Richard Light (1974) places the estimate between 200,000 and 500,000 cases of child abuse.

Although the data on the incidence of child abuse are not as well documented as those on criminal homicide because of problems of defining what constitutes abuse and of under-reporting of cases, there is sufficient evidence that each year a large number of parents beats, batters, and sometimes kills its offspring.

### Other Intrafamily Violence

There are few studies or other estimates about the phe-nomenon of nonlethal familial violence, particularly between a husband and wife. O'Brien has examined violence in divorce-prone families (1971). He reports that spontaneous mentions of overt violence occurred in 25 of 150 interviews (O'Brien, 1971: 694). A second study of families in the process of getting a divorce (Levinger, 1966) also examined the phenomenon of violence between spouses. Levinger's study found that physical abuse was an important factor in 20% of the middle- and 40% of the working-class cases. A third study, by Whitehurst (1971) focused on violently jealous husbands. Whitehurst's general discussion of this be-havior argued that there was a qualitative difference in social-ization of lower-class males and middle-class males in terms of the use of violence, but he provided no specific empirical data from his research.

### Beneath the Tip of the Iceberg

The evidence on family violence indicated by research on homicide, aggravated assault, child abuse, and nonlethal, non-criminally reported violence reveals that violence in the family is indeed widespread. However, these cases may be only the tip of the iceberg of family violence. While there has been little examination of forms of violence, such as wife pushing, or hitting between family members (we do not even know the simple fact of what proportion of husbands ever hit their wives or vice versa), it may be that these forms of violence are quite widespread. Part of the reason why this assumption is made is because if extreme forms of violence (murder and child abuse) can occur with such frequency, then it is likely that less extreme violence between family members is very common indeed! This research is aimed at the day-to-day patterned use of force and violence in families that escapes the public eye and has yet to be investigated.

## VIOLENCE AND THE FAMILY

Given the assumption of the prevalence of violence in the family and of the accompanying scarcity of research on husband-wife violence, there are some major issues that need to be answered in proposing a study of family violence. The first question concerns a conceptual definition of violence. Earlier in the chapter it was said that the focus of the research is on physical violence—beating, battering, slapping, shoving, pushing, or striking. There is, however, a major problem in defining what actually constitutes "violent" behavior as opposed to other modes of physical contact. Second, physical violence should be explained as a category of behavior that is conceptually distinct from "psychological" violence. A final issue concerns the study of violence in the family setting. Given the importance of studying violent behavior, the question remains, why study it in the family as opposed to studying violent acts irrespective of locale or relationship of the victim?

### Physical Violence
Defining "violence" to mean one individual hitting, striking, battering, assaulting, or throwing an object at another

person is questionable when dealing with violence in families. While there is probably agreement that a wife who stabs her husband has committed a violent act, there is little agreement as to whether a parent slapping a child's hands is being violent. One possible solution to the rather broad conceptualization of violence would be to separate "violence" from "force." Violence could be thought of as acts that society views as nonnormative, while force could be those acts that fall within society's definition of legitimate behavior such as disciplining children by spanking or slapping them. This "solution," however, opens up a Pandora's box of problems. Who decides which acts are legitimate and which are illegitimate? Is force hitting a child without physical evidence of injury, while violence is hitting a child and causing a black and blue mark? If one depends on a definition of situation to define what is violent—who defines the situation and when? Many of the respondents in this study were able to justify as nonviolent (?) even the most severe beating they received or administered after the act and after the bruises had healed.

The solution to the problem of defining the concept of "violence" employed in this research is to retain the broad conceptualization with the acknowledgment that there will be times when the term will be applied to acts (particularly those pertaining to parents striking children to discipline them) that are clearly *not ordinarily considered violent.* A further discussion of types of violence in Chapter 2 will deal with this issue in more detail.

Another issue in the study of physical violence is nonphysical or psychic violence. To focus on violence in its physical form does not mean that there are not other patterns of nonphysical violence that occur in the family. Indeed, as other research (Laing, 1969; Laing and Esterson, 1964) shows, and as some of our respondents indicated, there are numerous incidents of psychological or psychic violence that take place in families. Nevertheless, a major assumption of this research is that there is a distinct difference between physical violence and nonphysical violence (Etzioni, 1971:

712). This research therefore will examine nonphysical violence only in terms of its relationship to actual physical
attack, as in the case of verbal abuse precipitating a physical
assault.

## The Family

Having wrestled with the conceptualization of "violence,"
the next issue concerns what is meant by violence in *the
family*—that is how is "family" defined and what relationship
of attackers and victims will be examined? Second, there is
the question of why is violence between family members a
special case that needs separate investigation and theoretical
analysis?

The focus on physical attacks in this research is confined
to the nuclear family—violent attacks between husband and
wife and parent and child is the phenomenon to be investigated. There are numerous cases where members of the
extended family (aunts, uncles, in-laws, and so on) also are
involved in physical violence within the family, but these
cases are few compared to the extent of spousal and parental
violence. Gil, for instance, found that mothers and fathers
constituted 90% of the perpetrators of child abuse (1971:
641). Of the homicides where the victims had familial relationships to their slayers, the most frequent relationship was
conjugal (Wolfgang, 1958: 212).

As stated earlier, the major emphasis of this study is to
examine violence between husband and wife. This focus has
been selected because of the lack of empirical research on
this mode of violence. There are, however, other patterns of
family violence. This research also will pay some attention to
parent-child violence, but it will not discuss such modes as a
child assaulting his parents or sibling violence. There probably are many incidents of these types of violence in the
family (see, for example, Adelson, 1972 on sibling violence),
but for the moment the emphasis will be on physical violence
between husband and wife.

The final issue concerns the investigation of violence within the family as a special case of violence. Even though violence between family members is thought to be widespread, why study it as opposed to studying violence in general? Might it not be better to investigate the general phenomenon of violent acts and to develop or to verify a theory of interpersonal violence than to focus exclusively on violence between family members? There are a number of reasons why violence between family members is unique enough to be investigated apart from other forms of violent behavior.

First, all general theories need to be specified to apply to particular manifestations of the phenomenon they seek to explain. Therefore, in terms of violence in the family, there is a need to specify a theory or theories of violence in order to account for violent attacks *between family members.*

Second, the family is a social group that has characteristics that differentiate it from many other small groups. In the family, statuses and roles are assigned on the basis of age and sex rather than interest and competence. The family as a social group has a mixed sex composition, while other small groups where violence is found such as delinquent gangs (Cohen, 1955; Miller, 1958) do not. In addition, there are vast disparities between families in age of husband and wife during child-rearing years; thus, a study of family violence examines a cross-section of ages whereas studies of gang or subcultural violence might not.

There are conflicting normative expectations with respect to violence in the family. On the one hand, the family is a group that society looks to for love, gentleness, and solidarity. On the other hand, it is one of the very few groups to which society gives a clear right (and sometimes the obligation) to use physical force and restraint—as in the physical punishment of children. Moreover, there are other implicit rights to use violence vested in the family relationship, such as those that hold that a husband or a wife can, under some circumstances, hit each other (Stark and McEvoy, 1970).

As a social group, the family is differentiated from others

in that there is a long-term commitment to the group ("until death do us part") coupled with difficulty in leaving if not satisfied (emotional, interpersonal, and legal difficulty).

Last, the family is characterized by a high level of emotional involvement. Not only does this differentiate the family from other social groups, it may to a certain extent explain personal violence between family members. As Singer (1971: 4) states:

> the fact that the greatest personal violence occurs within the family suggests that aggressive behavior is more closely tied to the emotional consequences of frustration of hopes, images, and day to day stress among people who have important, complex relations.

## STUDYING FAMILY VIOLENCE

As I pointed out earlier, research on family violence is sparse considering the estimated incidence of child abuse, wife beating, family homicides, and other forms of physical violence that occur between family members in our society. One explanation for the paucity of research in this area is that the topic is extremely sensitive (see Farberow, 1966 for discussion of difficulties in research on "taboo" or sensitive topics). The possibility of social and legal reaction precludes discussing such behavior publicly or with one's intimates. There are possible problems of massive underreporting of incidents of violence both as a result of the desire to respond with a socially acceptable answer and the threat of legal sanctions. The possibility of underreporting is born out in the medical literature on child abuse, where physicians report extreme difficulty in getting parents to admit that they have physically abused their children (Kempe, 1962: 19). Many doctors are reluctant even to start asking questions about a possible case of abuse!

There are a variety of other problems faced by the researcher investigating a sensitive issue such as family violence.

Subjects may be embarrassed to talk about the behavior; they may become insulted by the researcher's technique, tone, or questions and refuse to continue; or, as was feared by Laud Humphreys when he studied homosexuality (1970: 41), the researcher who asks the wrong question may in the course of his research be beaten by subjects.

In light of the problems involved in researching a sensitive issue such as intrafamily violence, a key aspect of the research was to design a procedure that could be utilized successfully in exploring this topic. The technique chosen was the informal, unstructured interview. This section discusses the rationale used in developing the interview technique and the procedures to be used. The next section deals with how the subject sample was selected.

## THE INFORMAL INTERVIEW

There were a variety of reasons why the informal, unstructured interview technique was selected as the procedure to be used in gathering data on family violence. First, the informal technique is one which is often used in exploratory research (for example, see Rainwater, Coleman, and Handel, 1959; Hall, 1948; Cuber and Harroff, 1966; Komarovsky, 1967; Vidich and Bensman, 1968; Schatzman and Strauss, 1955). It has the advantage of not restricting the scope and content of the interview with extremely specific questions that call for exact answers. Because intrafamily violence is still an open issue theoretically, it was desirable not to constrain the nature of the data collected. The technique of open-ended informal questions allows the researcher to focus on the context in which the behavior occurs. As Cuber and Harroff (1966: 13) state, while the data collected are incomplete statistically, we gain information about what in his own life is important to the subject.

The use of the informal technique may open up new areas of the phenomenon that the researcher may not have considered when he began the study. After the first 20 inter-

views, interesting aspects of family violence were in fact
uncovered that had not been considered during the design
stage of the research. For instance, episodes of violence
seemed to cluster around holidays such as Christmas and New
Year's. Second, a number of wives reported being beaten
while pregnant.

In terms of researching sensitive areas, the use of the
informal procedure allows the researcher to approach the
topic of violence gradually. The interviewer can spend some
time at the beginning of the interview establishing rapport
with the respondent and slowly approach violence within the
respondent's own family. This reduced the likelihood of
respondents breaking off the interview or refusing to answer
particular questions.

### The "Funneling Technique"

The informal interview used in this research employed a
"funneling technique" to approach the issue of family violence. The interview schedule consisted of general questions
about respondents' family problems and solutions that family
members use to cope with these problems. In the first section, respondents were asked to discuss problems and solutions in friends' or neighbors' families. This provided an
opportunity to talk about any incidents of family violence
that the respondent knew about in other families. Sometimes, a respondent would mention his own family and
problems in response to questions about neighbors:

Interviewer:  In this neighborhood, has there ever been any police
              intervention in a family or family fight between
              parents or children?

Mrs. (51)[1]:  They came here.

Interviewer:  What was that about?

Mrs. (51):    Well, my problem was that my husband drank and it
              got to a point where it was unbearable and he was
              always coming home late and fighting . . . no matter

> what time he came in, it was loud and as long as he
> was hitting me, fine, but the children were getting
> older and of course they are awakened and he really
> abused . . . he'd take it out on the kids.

After discussing family problems of neighbors and friends,
the respondent was then asked questions about major problems that *his family* faces—problems between husband and
wife and problems between parents and children. From here,
a series of probe questions channeled the conversation
towards any incidents of violence that may have occurred in
the family. For instance, the interviewer may ask the
respondent to name the *most serious* problem his family
faces, or to describe one incident that occurred recently as an
example of a family problem. During these probe questions,
respondents often would begin to discuss problems that were
associated with violent attacks or would state that the problem was violent attacks. Sometimes, a respondent would
conclude that the probes were aimed at incidents of violence
and point-blank state that there were no such incidents:

Interviewer: What happens when you lose your temper?

Mrs. (43): I scream and holler . . . we never hit if that's what
you're trying to get at.

If there were no discussions of violence during the indirect
probe questions, the interviewer would then comment that a
number of families interviewed reported incidents where
members of the family hit each other and "has this occurred
in your family?" The precedent for this direct approach was
established in the Kinsey (Kinsey, Pomeroy, and Martin,
1948) study of sexual behavior. Kinsey (1948: 53) argues
that the burden of denial should be on the subject and that
the researcher should not make it easier for the subject to
deny the behavior. In researching the sensitive area of sexual
behavior, Kinsey assumed that everyone engaged in every
type of activity and asked direct questions. In the study of

family violence, the direct question often jarred the memory of the respondent and the discussion of violence commenced:

> Interviewer:  In the course of the interviews that we have done, we find that a husband and wife will push or shove each other in the course of an argument.

> Mrs. (46):  Oh, I forgot about that. . . . He's hit me a few times, slapped me.

> Interviewer:  When was the last time?

> Mrs. (46):  When I had the argument after Easter . . . that's why I wanted to leave him.

Thus, general questions and probe questions "funnel" the discussion in the direction of the issue under investigation— the incidence, types, and circumstances surrounding violence in the family.

The "funneling technique" worked well. It allowed the development of rapport with the respondent and seemed to produce little negative reaction on the part of respondents. They seemed to be able to discuss violent episodes more easily if the topic was gradually approached. No interviews were broken off. In some cases, the "funneling" did not progress very far before the issue of violence was brought up, while in other cases, only the direct statement about violence brought forth discussions or denials of violence.

## POPULATION AND SAMPLE

Once an instrument for gathering data had been decided on, the next problem was "who to interview?" Because this research is a study of families where violence is used by family members on family members, it was necessary to obtain a sufficient number of families to interview where violence occurred in order to meet the theoretical criteria of the research. At the time the research was first planned, physical violence between husband and wife was thought of as infrequent, perhaps in one out of ten marriages. A random sample of a population would be extremely cumbersome in terms of the methods of interviewing and the data analysis. The expense required to interview enough families to provide a sufficient number where violence occurred would have been prohibitive.[2]

Therefore, a focused sample of families where known incidents of violence had taken place was used. The rationale for this choice was two-fold. First, the investigation's efforts would be concentrated on families where violence is or has been used. Second, this sampling procedure provides a means of validating the results of the interview because there is evidence before the interview that the family has had experience with violence. Thus, there is a means of checking the responses to the interview with some other indicator. The sample of "violent families" was drawn from two sources—a private social work agency and the case log of a police department.

### Agency Cases

Agency cases were drawn from the files and with the cooperation of a private social work agency, Child and Family Services. The agency asked its caseworkers to review their case-loads and to list the names and addresses of families who may have reported incidents of physical violence where the caseworker observed or had been told about serious family conflict, marital disagreements, or parent-child conflict (see Appendix B for copy of the letter sent to caseworkers). The caseworkers were asked to indicate next to each name why the family was included (for example, wife reported, relatives reported, or "this was a hunch of mine").

In cooperation with the agency, the list was examined and a number of cases that were recent (during the past year) and were located within the city of Manchester, New Hampshire, were selected. Manchester was chosen because it was the only city where more than 20 cases were listed by the social workers.

Because of the agency's concern with the rights of clients and with confidentiality, the agency wished to obtain permission of the respondents before they were interviewed. Using the list of cases that met the selection criteria, the agency contacted individuals and asked for permission to interview them. Of those contacted, there were seven refusals. The final number of agency cases interviewed was 20.

It should be pointed out that not all of the 20 cases that were interviewed were selected because of an advance knowledge of husband-wife violence. In the first place, a number of these cases were included in the list because of "hunches" of caseworkers. Second, the agency was aware of the principal researcher's previous work on child abuse and included a number of families because of suspected parent-child violence. Thus, while the agency cases included a high number of families where there was some knowledge of conjugal violence, there was no guarantee that all 20 would evidence some or any incidents of violence between spouses. Families drawn from the agency will be referred to as "agency families" in the text and tables of the manuscript.

### Police "Blotter" Cases

Because it was felt that a sample drawn exclusively from the files of a private agency might reflect a middle-class bias, a second sample of 20 families was drawn from the "blotter" (the record of all police calls) of a police department. Because of the factors involved in the police being called in to intervene in family strife—such as close proximity of neighbors in apartments or houses—the police blotter sample was assumed to be predominantly urban and from the lower socioeconomic statuses.

While it would have been preferable to draw this sample from the police cases in Manchester, the lack of cooperation from this police department forced a change to Portsmouth, New Hampshire. All police calls coded "Family Troubles" and all cases coded "Assaults" were examined. The investigators compiled a list of cases where the police were called in to intervene in a family disturbance, family squabble, or actual physical assault between family members. The compilation of the pool of families was complicated by a number of factors. First, all cases involving juveniles had to be eliminated because of legal restrictions concerning access to police records dealing with juvenile offenses. Second, the files contained a large number of cases with no names of complainants, or unknown or unclear addresses. This made it impossible to include these cases because it could not be determined *who* should be interviewed. In order to have a large enough pool of families to interview (at least 25), some families had to be included where the file only indicated "family problem," or "family call."

During the interviewing, the pool of police cases was further diminished by the fact that a number of the addresses turned out to be fictitious or nonexistent. In addition, it became apparent either before an interview, or sometimes even during an interview, that the family listed in the police blotter was not the family that was at that residence. This was either the result of the family moving, or, in two of the instances, the family at the address in the police blotter was the one that had called the police to intervene for a neighbor who was having family problems.

Thus, as the pool became narrower and more families were included because of the general label of "family problem," the likelihood decreased that all cases of police intervention had histories of violence. Thus, as with the agency cases, while a large number of police blotter cases *did have* previously known incidents of violence, *not all* of the police blotter families interviewed were known to have or actually did have a history of family violence. The 20 families who were included in the sample because of police intervention will be referred to in the text and tables of the manuscript as "police families."

## Neighbors: No Known History of Violence

A major problem with some of the research on family violence, particularly research on child abuse, is that there is no attempt to compare samples of violent individuals—abusers—

with any comparative group of nonviolent individuals—nonabusers (Gelles, 1973: 614). In order to provide a means of comparing *known* violent families to families where there is no knowledge of any history of violent occurrences, a sample was drawn from the neighbors of the agency and the police families. Thus, for each family member interviewed from the agency files or police blotter, a neighbor family member was interviewed. These families were chosen using a systematic rotation schedule (that is, the interviewer selected a neighbor family either to the right, left, or across the street).

A sample of 40 neighbors (20 for police families, 20 for agency families) was interviewed. In the text and tables the neighbors of the agency clients will be referred to as "agency neighbors" and the neighbors of the police families will be referred to as "police neighbors."

We hoped that interviewing these families would provide data on the incidence of violence in the general population because it was expected that there would be some violence in these families even though they were not clients of an agency or had called the police to intervene in a family dispute.[3]

## THE INTERVIEWS

The 80 interviews were conducted over a nine-month period by two interviewers, one male (the author) and one female.[4] Each interviewer conducted 40 interviews and questioned half (10) of each of the four subgroups (agency families, agency neighbors, police families, police neighbors).

### Contacting the Subjects

As stated earlier, the agency families were contacted by agency caseworkers who requested their permission to be interviewed. The families that gave their permission were then asked to name a convenient day and time. The other 60 families were contacted at their homes by the interviewers and asked if they would take part in the research. The

families that consented either were interviewed immediately
or an appointment was made for a later date.

It had been decided that respondents would be either the
husbands or the wives, with the goal to be an almost even
number of each. It became apparent early in the research that
husbands would be quite difficult to interview. Even though
the interviewers varied the time and days that they conducted the interviews, few husbands were available or would
consent to be interviewed.[5] Other researchers (Snell, Rosenwald, and Robey, 1964) have found that husbands are unwilling to be interviewed about incidents of family violence. At
one point, joint interviews were attempted with both husband and wife in order to increase husband participation.
These, however, flirted with disaster as some altercations
almost arose during the joint interviews:

Interviewer:  You made up after that argument?

Mrs. (3):     Yeah.

Mr. (3):      I'd forgotten all about that one.

Mrs. (3):     I didn't!

*     *     *

Interviewer:  What does your wife do that upsets you?

Mr. (60):     Let's see, what does she do. . . .

Mrs. (60):    Tell the truth so I can find out.

Mr. (60):     I'll tell the truth . . . I'll tell the truth. Uh, she's a
              very neat person, and I am not. And a lot of times
              that comes first. The place has got to be perfectly
              neat and tidy, and once in a while it gets on my
              nerves.

Mrs. (60):    That's right, and you better clean the closet and the
              shed.

\* \* \*

Interviewer: What was the most serious punishment you ever
received?

Mrs. (60):    I got one spanking in my life.

Mr. (60):     You should have gotten more!

After abandoning the joint interview method as a procedure that potentially might precipitate family violence instead of studying it, it was decided that the respondent ought
to be the spouse who would be the best informant. Therefore, no attempt was made to pressure a husband into being
the respondent if he were home with his wife and reluctant
to talk. The final result was 66 wives interviewed and 14
husbands.

A second problem in contacting subjects is one which is
endemic to the door-to-door interview: finding people home
and gaining their permission to be interviewed. This problem
existed for the 60 families (police families, their neighbors,
and agency neighbors) where no previous appointment to be
interviewed was possible. It was obvious that the interviewer
could not knock on the door and simply ask if the person
wanted to discuss family *violence.* Therefore, interviewers
introduced the topic of the research by stating that the
research dealt with family problem solving. A letter to the
effect also was presented (see Appendix B). Second, the
interviewer assured the potential respondent of the confidentiality of the interview. Even with interviewer persistence
and prepared introductions, there were a number of people
who were not at home or who simply were not interested in
being interviewed. Of the police blotter cases, 17 potential
subjects simply were unavailable, while three families refused
to participate. In sampling neighboring families, for *each*
interview completed the average number of neighbors not at
home when the interviewer knocked on the door was four,
while the average number of refusals to participate was three.

There was one neighborhood where an unusual number of

people refused to be interviewed. Finally, when one family consented they told the interviewer of a story that seemed to account for the wariness of the neighborhood:

Mr. (60):    Well, a few weeks ago there was this guy who came knocking on the doors in the neighborhood. He said he was a biology student at the University and was doing research on anatomy. He said he wanted to take pictures . . . nude pictures of the boys in the family. So finally, someone called the police and they got this guy. It turns out he was some nut who wasn't from the University at all!

## Conducting the Interviews

Most of the interviews were conducted in the homes of the respondents. Two interviews with agency cases took place in the agency—one because a husband did not want his wife to know he was being interviewed, one because the interview occurred during a wife's lunch hour. Another interview was done at the place of work of the respondent. It was felt that the home would be the best location for the interview because the respondent would be more likely to be relaxed there. In addition, it allowed the interviewer to gather some data on the condition of the home and the family's life style. An added "bonus" in some interviews was the opportunity to watch respondent-child interaction. A number of mothers spanked or hit their children during the course of the interview.

Because of the open-ended, informal interview format, it was felt that it would be necessary to tape record all the interviews. In order to reduce respondents' negative reactions, a small unobtrusive tape recorder (Craig Model 2605) with a built-in microphone was used. This recorder is about the size of a package of cigars and each respondent was asked if the recorder could be used. Of the 80, only three people refused permission to be recorded.[6] Unlike previous research where it was reported that taping equipment made respondents uncomfortable (Komarovsky, 1967: 12), none of the respondents seemed to be, or stated that he or she was bothered by, the presence of the tape recorder (although one individual asked if the recorder could be turned off for a portion of the interview.

The interviews lasted an hour to an hour and a half. Sometimes discussions continued even after the "formal" interview ended and the recorder was turned off. When this occurred, the interviewer dictated these discussions onto the tape after he left the house. Because the interviewing began without actually informing the respondent of the specific investigation underway (family violence), it was necessary to inform the respondent at the end of the interview what that specific topic was. Often this was not necessary as the respondent had figured out what the interviewer was seeking during the probe questions. There seemed to be no concern on the part of respondents; and they agreed that the interviewer would have had problems if he had announced the specific intent of the interview at the door-step.

### Why Would Anyone Tell You About THAT?

Throughout the design stage of the research and well into the interviews themselves, people such as the chief of police of Manchester, social workers, and others reacted to the proposed research by shaking their heads and saying, "Why would anyone tell you about *that?*" Having completed the 80 interviews, many of which involved the respondent discussing incidents of violence and other personal aspects of family life, the question still remains—why *did* they tell us about *that?*

What makes, or what causes, people to reveal to absolute strangers quite personal incidents in their life is probably an empirical question in its own right. As far as this research was concerned, the answer seems to be how the respondents perceived the interviewers. A number of respondents commented that the interviewer was one of the few people who knew about their problems.

Mrs. (6):     Well, if I was talking to somebody I didn't know, like everybody thinks we're perfectly happy. And

> there is only Mrs. Gregor (a social worker), my
> girlfriend, and you, and my doctor that knows the
> difficulties that we are having. As far as my neigh-
> bors, anybody else, we're an ideal family, very
> happy. But, how I feel, like I tell Mrs. Gregor, I've
> accepted it the way it is. Sometimes I get depressed.
> Ah, I get very nervous, and sometimes I feel as
> though I wish I had somebody to talk to and discuss
> it with me. But, if I can get through that day, then
> the next day, things look a little better and I can
> continue from there.

Mrs. (6) seems to articulate some of the reasons why
people spoke with us. In the first place, many of the respondents were desperate for people to talk to about their problems. They seemed to look at the interviewer as a confidant,
whom they did not have. The interviewer was taken to be a
combination confidant-social worker who would keep everything private.

Mrs. (69):   You said this is confidential, right. . . . Unbeknown
to anyone, I went to a psychiatric social worker . . .
the year before last. I went for 3 months. I snuck up
and snuck back. My husband never knew, neither
did anyone else.

It seemed that the fact that the interviewer was a stranger
and did not know the actors or events to which the respondent referred made it easier for the respondent to open up.

Mrs. (61):   I find it easy to talk with you because I don't know
you and I know you aren't going to gossip or tell
anyone what I said. You don't know my family so
it's a lot easier to tell you.

Strangers, people who don't know the family, appear to be
considered objective, and thus could be counted on to give an
impartial judgment of the family's problems. One respondent
thought that the interviewer would be a good person to have
talk to her husband to "straighten him out."

Interviewer: Who would you have liked to talk with your husband?

Mrs. (51):   Well, like for yourself . . . you're a pure stranger . . .
perhaps if you had told him, "well you want to be
married or don't you . . . either you live at home
and support your family . . . don't you want to be a
man?" Perhaps it would have helped.

In addition, some respondents displayed a willingness to
cooperate and help the study in any way they could.

Mrs. (78):   About 3 or 4 years ago I was living with a boy and
got pregnant. And I found out he just wasn't the
one . . . long hair and doing drugs. When I got pregnant I was more aware. I didn't want him for a
husband or a father for my kid. So I just drifted
away and met Al, my husband. And he knew of
course that I was pregnant . . . I was sticking out
like a balloon. And we just started going together.
Finally, I had her and I had her under his name even
though we weren't married . . . but we were living
together. She was a year old when I got pregnant
with Sandy and we decided we better get married. I
don't know if this is helping whatever you are
doing, but that's what happened.

Mrs. (58):   Well, I never told anyone this, not even my caseworker, but if it will help what you are studying . . .
the one I'm pregnant with now is not from my
husband.

Thus, because they wanted someone to talk to, they
trusted the interviewer, they hoped the interviewer would see
things their way or might know how to help them, or they
wanted to help the interviewers in what they were doing,
respondents sat back and discussed their private married lives,
their problems, and incidents of physical violence.

Appendix A presents a demographic profile of the subjects

and also discusses the strengths and weaknesses of the sampling technique in light of these data.

## OBJECTIVE OF THE RESEARCH

The objective of this research is to study the causes, incidence, and types of physical violence used by spouses on each other. Data on the use of violence by parents on children also are presented.

Chapter 2 presents descriptive data concerning the nature and extent of violence between family members. The first section presents data on the overall incidence of violence within the families of the respondents. The second section develops a typology of intrafamily violence based on the meanings attached by the family members to incidents of violence. The chapter concludes with an eight-fold typology of violence built around three dimensions of physical violence: 1) Instrumental-Expressive, 2) Legitimate-Illegitimate, 3) Victim-precipitated/Not-victim-precipitated.

Chapter 3 examines the violent situation by focusing on temporal patterns, spatial patterns, and presence or absence of other people. A major portion of this chapter concerns the association of alcohol and violence.

The violent family's location in the social structure and the structure of the violent family are analyzed in Chapter 4. Aspects of family life such as social position (education, occupation, income, age), religion, social isolation, family size, and unwanted pregnancy are examined in terms of their relation to violence. This chapter proposes that certain positions in the social structure and particular family structures produce stress that can lead to incidents or patterns of intrafamily violence.

Chapter 5 suggests that the victim plays an important part in the attack or violence. A detailed discussion is presented dealing with the interaction between victim and offender that leads to an attack.

Chapter 6 proposes that the family is a "training ground for violence" and discusses how violence and approval of violence are learned in early childhood. This chapter discusses how role models for family violence presented in early childhood are translated into actual violence in later family life.

Chapter 7, the final chapter, integrates the theoretical discussions in the previous chapters into a unified theoretical model of intrafamily violence.

## NOTES

1. Respondents and their families will be identified in the text with numbers corresponding to their interview numbers. This system is used so that particular individuals and families can be referred to throughout the text.

2. The expense might have been prohibitive because a large number of families might have had to have been interviewed in order to provide a sufficient number of families where violence occurred. Although it was assumed in the first chapter that violence is fairly common, there is no information on how common it actually is. Thus, in order to get a sample of families where violence occurs, well over 200 families might have had to have been interviewed using a random sample design.

3. It must be pointed out that because there was no attempt to make this sample of neighbors representative of any general population, any generalizations made about the incidence of violence must be considered speculative and subject to more rigorous examination. Also, this sampling procedure made no attempt to match neighbors to agency or police families on any criteria other than they be married (or previously married) and that they live in the same neighborhood.

4. The male interviewer is white, 27 years old, and was a graduate student at the University of New Hampshire while the interviews were carried out. The female interviewer is white, 22 years old, and had graduated from the University of New Hampshire with a major in Social Service prior to beginning her work as an interviewer. Both conducted pilot interviews as part of their training in the use of the conversational interview technique. The author had had previous experience in this method of data collecting.

5. Divorce, legal separation, ad hoc separation, husband's working hours, husband's reluctance to talk, and a variety of other factors led to the husband's lack of availability. In many cases when the husband and wife were both home, the husband insisted that he be left out and that

his wife talk for the family. Even in the interviews where the husband participated, if the wife was home she often joined in and even sometimes dominated the remainder of the interview.

6. In addition, four interviews were lost because of faulty or inoperative taping equipment. The content of these interviews was written from memory by the interviewer shortly after the completion of the interview.

*Chapter 2*

# INCIDENCE, METHODS, AND MEANINGS OF

# INTRAFAMILY VIOLENCE

The bits and pieces of relevant research provide few clues as to how much intrafamily violence there is in our society. We have no data on the incidence of conjugal violence (except homicide) and the data on child abuse are, at best, questionable. There is no available material that suggests whether violence between family members consists of isolated events or whether it occurs in some families on a patterned and frequent basis. Further, we tend to think of violence as a unitary phenomenon, even though there may be different types of violence occurring in families with different meanings attached to the incidents by family members.

The examination of intrafamily violence begins in this chapter with an overview of violence between family members. The first section reports the incidence of conjugal violence and parent-to-child violence in the overall sample of 80 and then compares the agency families, police families, and their neighbors. This section also presents the frequency of various methods of violent attacks (slapping, punching, choking, and so on) that occur between husband and wife and parent and child.

The second section of the chapter provides an intensive view of family violence by examining the meanings attached to the incidents of violence by family members. It becomes obvious that violence is not a unitary phenomenon (Corning and Corning, 1972: 10); there are several kinds of physical violence. Violence varies according to the context in which it is used; according to the meaning of the act to both the actors, the family, and the community; and according to how family members account (Lyman and Scott, 1970) for different acts of violence. The types of violence set forth here are based on how actors account for acts of violence and what these acts mean to them and their families. The final section develops an eight-fold typology of family violence and discusses the variety of perspectives from which family violence can be viewed and defined.


## FAMILY VIOLENCE: INCIDENCE AND METHODS

### Conjugal Violence

A major purpose for undertaking this research was to evaluate the idea that physical violence between husband and wife is much more common than is generally realized. This notion became stronger as the research developed. In the first ten interviews, four of the respondents reported at least some occurrence of conjugal violence. The accuracy of this guess essentially was demonstrated in the first tabulation of the data, which showed that over half of the 80 families interviewed described one or more instances where husband or wife pushed, kicked, or in some manner used physical violence on his or her spouse. Moreover, of these 44 families using violence, 21 (or 26% of the entire sample) were participants in husband-wife assaults on a *regular* basis, ranging from half a dozen times a year to every day (Table 1).

TABLE 1
## PERCENT OF TOTAL CONJUGAL VIOLENCE BY
## SOURCE OF RESPONDENT

| | Total Spouse Violence | | | | | |
|---|---|---|---|---|---|---|
| | None | Threat | Once | Seldom* | Regular Low** | Regular High*** |
| Agency Families (N=20) | 40 | 0 | 10 | 20 | 20 | 10 |
| Agency Neighbors (N=20) | 65 | 5 | 5 | 10 | 10 | 5 |
| Police Families (N=20) | 15 | 0 | 10 | 25 | 20 | 30 |
| Police Neighbors (N=20) | 55 | 0 | 15 | 20 | 0 | 10 |
| Total (N=80) | 44 | 1 | 10 | 19 | 12 | 14 |

*2 to 5 times in marriage
**from twice a year to once every other month
***from once a month to daily

As expected, because of the way in which these families were selected, the police families were the ones with the most conjugal violence. Seventeen (85%) had at least one incident of violence. (Of the three families who called the police when there was no violence, one called to report the death of a neighbor and the other two called about suspected vandalism in their neighborhood.) In half of the police families, while there was violence on a regular basis, the police were called for only one of a number of incidents of violence in that family during the past year.

The lowest incidence of violence occurred among the neighbors of the agency cases. Only three of these families (15%) used violence regularly and another three reported occasional violence. Thus, as compared to the 60% of the agency cases who reported one or more incidents, only 30% of their neighbors reported such events.

The neighbors of the police and agency families provide the opportunity to examine the incidence of violence in families where there is no public record of violence (police not called in to intervene), no agency contact, and no publicly known marital difficulty (no applicants for divorce and no litigants in divorce cases).[1] In the neighbor families, 15 (37%) had at least one incident of violence between husband and wife, while violence was a regular occurrence in five families (12%). The 37% figure of one or more conjugal assaults falls between the figures cited by Levinger (1966) in his study of applicants for divorce who complained of physical abuse (20% of middle-class families and 40% working-class families complained of physical abuse).

Although the neighbor families provide an insight into how extensive family violence is, it is possible that the incidence reported is lower than the actual occurrence. In the first place, this group excludes all those families where the police were called in to mediate violent fights and it excludes families who seek help from social work agencies and report incidents of violence. In the second place, while the interview was designed to enhance the establishment of rapport and reduce underreporting, there still may be a number of respondents who were reluctant to discuss or admit to any incidents of violence. Finally, because the interview was structured around family problems and family problem solving, a certain number of incidents of violence may not have been reported because the respondent did not believe that being hit or hitting under certain circumstances constitutes a family problem. Although the direct questioning should have reduced this possibility of nonreporting, some respondents may have decided that some physical contacts were just cases of "playing around" or "fooling around" and were not really incidents of "real violence."[2]

The statistics on violence in the neighbor families presented here and in later sections should be interpreted and used with caution because we actually interviewed only one of every ten neighbors we tried to contact. Thus, the neighbor sample is not at all representative of any population.

*Husband to Wife.* The husband is the more violent of marital partners. Twenty-nine husbands (47%) hit their wives at least once, while 20 (25%) hit their wives from six times a year to daily (Table 2). The police family husbands were the most violent: 15 (75%) have hit their wives and half hit their wives regularly. The least violent husbands were the agency neighbors—only four (20%) ever hit their wives. In the neighbor families, 12 husbands (30%) hit their wives at least once and of these, eight (20%) hit their wives frequently.

### TABLE 2
### PERCENT OF HUSBAND TO WIFE AND WIFE TO HUSBAND VIOLENCE BY SOURCE OF RESPONDENT

|  | Violence | | | | | |
|---|---|---|---|---|---|---|
|  | None | Threat | Once | Seldom* | Regular Low** | Regular High*** |
| **Agency Families:** | | | | | | |
| Husband to wife (N=20) | 45 | 0 | 10 | 20 | 15 | 10 |
| Wife to husband (N=20) | 75 | 0 | 0 | 15 | 5 | 5 |
| **Agency Neighbors:** | | | | | | |
| Husband to wife (N=20) | 75 | 5 | 5 | 0 | 10 | 5 |
| Wife to husband (N=20) | 75 | 0 | 0 | 10 | 10 | 5 |
| **Police Families:** | | | | | | |
| Husband to wife (N=20) | 25 | 0 | 5 | 20 | 20 | 30 |
| Wife to husband (N=20) | 45 | 0 | 20 | 15 | 5 | 15 |
| **Police Neighbors:** | | | | | | |
| Husband to wife (N=20) | 60 | 0 | 25 | 5 | 0 | 10 |
| Wife to husband (N=20) | 75 | 0 | 10 | 15 | 0 | 0 |
| **Total:** | | | | | | |
| Husband to wife (N=80) | 51 | 1 | 11 | 11 | 11 | 14 |
| Wife to husband (N=80) | 67 | 0 | 8 | 14 | 5 | 6 |

*2 to 5 times in marriage
**from twice a year to once every other month
***from once a month to daily

*Wife to Husband.* Although the wives were less violent than their husbands, they were far from passive. Twenty-six (32%) have hit their husbands. Of these, nine (11%) hit their husbands from at least a half a dozen times a year to as much as daily. The police wives were the most violent—11 (55%) hit their husbands at least once, and of these, four (20%) were regular protagonists in violent episodes. Agency wives were less violent—only five (25%) ever struck their husbands. In the neighbor families, eight wives (20%) struck their husbands and three of these hit their husbands more than occasionally (Table 2).

It would appear that in the high violence families (those who called the police), violence is not just the case of one spouse hitting the other, but there is evidence of general violence with both partners being offenders as well as victims. In the lesser violent families, the husband is usually the aggressor while the wife hits back or initiates an attack less frequently. Chapter 4, which examines violence and family structure, will further discuss these findings by analyzing the interactive aspects of family violence.

*Methods of Conjugal Violence.* Within the 44 families where violence took place, there was a variety of violent attacks ranging from pushing and shoving to assault with a knife. Table 3 presents the methods of violence used by husbands and wives.

The most common mode of violence is slapping, scratching, or grabbing the other person. Husbands predominate in violence that requires the physical dominance of the attacker over the victim such as pushing, pushing (downstairs, for instance) or choking. Many wives argue that they cannot match their husbands in physical strength, and thus, when they initiate attacks or retaliate, they do so in the extreme. The only individual who actually stabbed a spouse was a wife, and the wives outnumbered the husbands four to two in hitting the victim with a hard object such as a lamp, lead pipe, or chair. That wives outnumber husbands in the use of some extreme forms of violence corresponds to Wolfgang's data (1957). In addition, the fact that the wives may use a

TABLE 3

## PERCENT OF HUSBANDS AND WIVES WHO EVER USED VIOLENCE ON EACH OTHER BY METHOD OF VIOLENCE

| VIOLENT ACT | Husband (N=80) | Wife (N=80) |
|---|---|---|
| Push or Shove | 18 | 1 |
| Throw an Object | 22 | 11 |
| Slap, Hit with Open Hand, Scratch, Grab | 32 | 20 |
| Punch or Kick | 25 | 9 |
| Push Down | 4 | 0 |
| Hit with Hard Object | 3 | 5 |
| Choke | 9 | 0 |
| Use Knife | 0* | 1 |
| Use Gun | 0** | 0 |

*1 husband threatened wife with knife
**3 husbands threatened wife with gun

knife but never a gun (while three husbands did threaten their wives with guns) corresponds to Pittman and Handy (1964: 465) in their study of assault where it was found that white females use knives more than guns.

### Parental Violence

The act of a parent hitting a child is so pervasive in our society that it is quite problematic to say that a parent who hits his child is being violent. In the 78 families with children there were reports of one or both parents hitting their children in 74 (96%) of the cases. Hitting a child is at least a monthly occurrence in 35 families (45%), and it is a daily affair in 10 of the 78 families (13%) with children (Table 4).

We expected that the agency clients would be the most physically aggressive towards their children. A large number of these families were included in the sample because the social workers knew that these families had serious parent-child problems. Physical aggression is a daily occurrence in five agency families (25%) and it occurs monthly or weekly

**TABLE 4**
## PERCENT OF TOTAL PARENTAL VIOLENCE
## BY SOURCE OF RESPONDENT

| | Total Parental Violence | | | | |
|---|---|---|---|---|---|
| | None | Once | Seldom** | Regular Low*** | Regular High**** |
| Agency Families (N=20) | 5 | 0 | 25 | 45 | 25 |
| Agency Neighbors (N=19)* | 5 | 11 | 58 | 21 | 5 |
| Police Families (N=20) | 0 | 5 | 35 | 40 | 20 |
| Police Neighbors (N=19)* | 5 | 0 | 74 | 21 | 0 |
| Total (N=78) | 4 | 4 | 47 | 32 | 13 |

*1 family had no children
**less than 6 times a year
***from once a month to once a week
****from daily to numerous times a day

in another nine families (45%)—thus, in 14 agency families (70%) children are hit regularly.

The police families were slightly less physically aggressive towards their children than agency families. There was no evidence in advance of any parent-child violence in the police families (they were selected because of known or suspected incidents of conjugal violence). Parents strike their children regularly in 12 families (60%). For four of these families, violence takes place daily or numerous times a day.

The police neighbors were the least physical parents—in no family were children hit daily and only four parents (21%) hit their children as much as once a month. The interviews with the neighbors of the police and agency families revealed that children are not hit solely in families with known husband-wife or parent-child difficulties. In 36 of 38 neighbor families (95%), children had been hit at least once. However, the frequency of violence in these families is lower than in the police or agency families. Only 22 of the neighbor parents (28%) hit their children once a month or more and only four of the 38 (11%) neighbor-parents hit their children on a daily basis.

*Mother to Child.* The most physically aggressive parent is the mother. Seventy-three of the mothers (94%) struck their children one or more times. More than half of these mothers (36) hit their children at least monthly and 11 (14%) hit their offspring daily (Table 5). That the mothers are violent towards their children corresponds to the finding in the child abuse literature that mothers abuse children as frequently or more frequently than fathers (Resnick, 1969: 327; Steele and Pollock, 1968: 107; Zalba, 1971; Gil, 1971: 641).

The most violent group of mothers were the agency clients. Fourteen (70%) struck their children regularly and of these, five mothers hit their children daily. The least violent mothers were the neighbors of these agency clients. Only five agency-neighbor mothers (26%) struck their children more than six times during the year. Mothers in the neighbor families hit their children (35 of 38 [92%] hit them on one or more occasions); however, they hit them less frequently than do the agency or police mothers.

*Father to Child.* While almost all the mothers hit their children, only 51 fathers (65%) ever struck their children. Of these 51, less than half hit their children monthly and only four hit their children daily (Table 5).

The agency fathers are the most aggressive (as are the agency mothers). Over half of these fathers hit their children regularly—anywhere from monthly to daily. Three fathers who hit their children regularly do so on a daily basis. The police fathers are the least violent—only five (25%) physically strike their children regularly, none hits them daily, and nine (45%) have never struck their children.

The neighbor families had a low level of paternal violence. Here 16 of 38 fathers (42%) hit their children only occasionally and only six of 38 (16%) hit their children more than once a month.

**TABLE 5**
**PERCENT OF FATHER AND MOTHER TO CHILD**
**VIOLENCE BY SOURCE OF RESPONDENT**

| | Violence | | | | |
|---|---|---|---|---|---|
| | None | Once | Seldom** | Regular Low*** | Regular High**** |
| **Agency Families:** | | | | | |
| Fathers (N=20) | 25 | 0 | 20 | 40 | 15 |
| Mothers (N=20) | 5 | 0 | 25 | 45 | 25 |
| **Agency Neighbors:** | | | | | |
| Fathers (N=19)* | 37 | 5 | 42 | 11 | 5 |
| Mothers (N=19)* | 16 | 5 | 53 | 21 | 5 |
| **Police Families:** | | | | | |
| Fathers (N=20) | 45 | 0 | 30 | 25 | 0 |
| Mothers (N=20) | 0 | 5 | 30 | 40 | 25 |
| **Police Neighbors:** | | | | | |
| Fathers (N=19)* | 32 | 5 | 47 | 16 | 0 |
| Mothers (N=19)* | 5 | 0 | 74 | 21 | 0 |
| **Total:** | | | | | |
| Fathers (N=78) | 35 | 3 | 35 | 23 | 5 |
| Mothers (N=78) | 6 | 3 | 45 | 32 | 14 |

*1 family had no children
**less than 6 times a year
***from once a month to once a week
****from daily to numerous times a day

*Methods of Parental Violence.* The span of parental violence includes slapping the child on the hand; spankings; spankings using objects such as teflon spoons, curtain rods, shoes, and so on; hitting the child with a hard object such as a bat or bicycle chain; and choking the child (Table 6).

In terms of the methods of parental violence, mothers are more violent than fathers for every mode of violent attack except for punching. As with conjugal violence, it seems that the female is reluctant to engage in interpersonal violence that involves doubling up a fist and actually punching another person—be it her husband or child.

## TABLE 6
## PERCENT OF MOTHERS AND FATHERS WHO EVER USED
## VIOLENCE ON THEIR CHILDREN BY METHOD OF VIOLENCE

| VIOLENT ACT | Father (N=78) | Mother (N=78) |
|---|---|---|
| Spank on Bottom | 60 | 92 |
| Spank using Object | 19 | 28 |
| Slap on Body | 13 | 21 |
| Slap in Face | 5 | 14 |
| Slam or Push into Wall | 0 | 3 |
| Punch | 3 | 1 |
| Hit with Hard Object | 1 | 1 |
| Choke | 0 | 1 |

## MEANINGS OF INTRAFAMILY VIOLENCE

As there are various *methods* of violence, there are different *meanings* attached to violent incidents by family members. The purpose of this section is not to produce an extensive typology of violence, but rather to discuss violence in terms of how the participants account for violent episodes and what violence means to them. Out of this accounting scheme emerges a number of types of violence.

The key aspect of this presentation is how the family members account for incidents or sequences of violent acts. Lyman and Scott (1970) provide the initial rationale for focusing on family members' accounts. "Accounts" are statements made by social actors to explain unanticipated or untoward behavior (Lyman and Scott, 1970: 112). Lyman and Scott (1970: 112) argue that nonroutine events require them. Although violence may be common in a family, it is still nonroutine and deviant by societal standards. Thus, its occurrence in a family necessitates an account either to explain or justify what happened. When the respondents discussed violence during the interviews, they were in reality "accounting" for its occurrence in their family.

From the respondents we learned that there were numerous incidents of violence in the family that were considered normal, routine, and needed little justification. These occurrences of "normal violence" were felt to be legitimate and even necessary for the family to exist. On the other hand, there were nonnormal acts of violence that were considered illegitimate and nonroutine. Different types of nonroutine violence began to emerge.

Before beginning the presentation of the types of family violence, it is first necessary to point out a major issue in our discussion of the meanings of violence. The fact that the majority of the interviews were with wives means that the typing of violence discussed in the following pages will reflect their perspective. In terms of husband-wife violence, we see violence mainly from the "victim's" point of view because wives are more likely to be victims of rather than committers of violence. In discussions of parent-child violence, the perspective is that of the main offender, the mother.

## Normal Violence

There are numerous incidents of violence in the family that are routine, normative, and even thought of as necessary by family members. These incidents constitute the type "Normal Violence." Normally approved violence is found both in cases of husband-wife violence and parent-child violence. Stark and McEvoy (1970: 52), in their analysis of the National Commission on the Causes and Prevention of Violence data, found that nearly one-fifth of all Americans approve of slapping one's spouse on appropriate occasions. Parnas (1967: 952), in his experience with police intervention in family quarrels, observed some occasions where wives believed that a husband should beat his wife "every once in a while."

Turning to parent-child violence, there is considerable support for certain types of normal violence towards children. Stark and McEvoy (1970: 54) found general approval for the use of strong discipline (usually physical force) on children by their parents. Blumberg (1964) also has discussed violence towards children and states that much of this violence is considered normal.

In short, normal violence is violence that is accepted, approved, and even mandated in family interaction. Parents and cultural norms articulate that "sparing the rod will spoil the child," while husbands and wives often regard as "all right" and acceptable a husband hitting his wife. From the point of view of the offender, normal violence is normal because it is instrumental in achieving or accomplishing some goal. The victim often believes that violence is acceptable because somehow he or she either deserved to be hit or benefited from being hit. Where normal violence occurs, it occurs with the approval of family members (however, sometimes approval comes after the act) and the level of violence is subscribed to as correct by the family.

*Husband-Wife: "I asked for it."* Normal violence in husband-wife interaction predominantly is violence where the husband is the aggressor and the wife the victim. Wives tend to believe that they are struck occasionally because they deserve it.

> Mrs. (75):  He hit me once. It wasn't very long ago. The baby was about 2 months old—July—we were fighting about something. I have a habit of not keeping my mouth shut. I keep at him and at him. He finally turned around and belted me. It was my fault, I asked for it.

Wives often accept being struck. They feel that they deserved to be hit because they precipitated the attack by badgering or nagging their husbands. Victim-precipitated violence often is normalized by the wife, who states that because she caused it, she deserved to be hit.

Mrs. (45):   It's over and I always seem to heal. I always looked
             at myself and said that I caused it in a way—it takes
             two. If I don't keep aggravating and aggravating it
             won't happen. I have to be honest where it lies. I, in
             a way, invited it so you can't turn around and
             condemn somebody. . . . If he came up to me out of
             the clear blue sky then I could say he was wrong.

Mrs. (45) has identified two major aspects of normal
conjugal violence. First, she believes that she somehow
caused it. If there had been no provocation on her part she
would not have accepted being hit. Second, the fact that she
"healed" contributes to an after-the-act definition of the
situation of violence being "normal." Some wives discussed
incidents of frequent and often serious physical violence
between them and their husbands and were able to accept the
violence either because they were not seriously damaged (no
broken bones) or because black and blue marks go away and
they "heal."

Some wives, while they don't believe in the act of hitting,
justify violence because it is a way in which their husbands
relieve tension. Wives seem to feel that a minimal level of
violence will prevent the buildup of pressure that might
provoke a more serious attack.

Mrs. (13):   Yea, you know. People should, you know. To me I
             think it's a good idea couples fighting or something.
             Like my husband has hit me before. Right, I don't
             believe in him hitting me but at the time if he
             hadn't done it, you know, this would have been on
             his head, you know, like, he has only hit me once
             and I think I deserved it—he thought I was cheating
             on him, but the position I was in I would have
             thought the same of him.

*Husband-Wife: "I tried to knock her to her senses."* A
second variety of normal conjugal violence is where the
offender justifies the violence based on it doing some good

for the victim. The classic case of this was the husband who, while he stated he never was violent with his wife, did slap her around to "knock her to her senses."

Mr. (53):    I have slapped her in the arm or in the face a few
             times to shut her up. Not really in an argument, it's
             usually when the kids get hurt. She just goes com-
             pletely spastic. She just doesn't know what to do.
             She just goes wild so you've got to hit her or
             something to calm her down so she'll come to her
             senses. I had to kick her out in a snow bank once to
             take care of my son when he cut his face. He slashed
             the whole side of his face and the blood was just
             gushing out and it was real bad. She kept screaming
             so I slapped her in the face, pushed her out in the
             snow bank, and when I got done patching my son
             she came back in the house. It's not because I'm
             mad at her, not because I'm trying to hurt her
             because of something she has done. I'm trying to
             knock her to her senses more or less. Another time
             she went wild and I took her in the hall for a few
             minutes and when I wrapped my son's finger up she
             came back in the house—it didn't look bad so she
             was all right, but I had to slap her face and hit her
             arm to calm her down.

This discussion brings to light what Stark and McEvoy (1970) call the "appropriate occasions" where slapping one's spouse is approved. Wives believe that their husbands were justified in hitting them when they brought on the attack by nagging their husbands. Some families feel that a certain level of violence is acceptable to relieve pressure, while other families use violence to control or calm down a hysterical spouse.

*Parent-Child: "Kids need to be hit."* The use of physical force by parents on their children is perhaps as common as "Doctor Dentons." In the 80 families interviewed, nearly all the parents hit their children at least once. Stark and McEvoy

(1970: 54) state that 84% of American parents have spanked their children. This use of physical force by parents on children is not only approved but mandated. The famous homily "spare the rod and spoil the child" is bolstered by other societal signposts that instruct parents that violence is a useful and necessary tool in childrearing. One such indicator was a slip the author found in a fortune cookie that pronounced: "The bamboo stick makes a good child."

That some violence towards children is normal is articulated by the parents who state that they only hit their children when they (the children) *need it* or *deserve to be hit.*

Mrs. (56):   Well, if they do something that they've been told over and over again that's it—well I don't say that to the little one, because she's kind of little. But once in a while, if they do something they know that it's really wrong, and I catch them doing it, well, then they deserve a spanking.

Mrs. (18):   Once in a great while I use a strap. I don't believe in hitting in the head or in the face—although Rhoda, I slapped her in the face a couple of times because she was sassing. *That* she needed.

Mrs. (59):   I spank her once a week—when she deserves it— usually when she is eating. I believe a child should eat so much and that is it.

When they use force, parents believe that they are doing some good for the child. This leads to the other standard homily of parent-child violence—"this is going to hurt *me* more than it does *you.*" Parents indicate that it is difficult but necessary to physically hit their children. It is necessary because of the harm that they believe can come to the children if they are not adequately disciplined. A number of parents who subscribe to the use of force felt that if their own parents had been more strict with them, they would not have had so many problems when they grew up.

Mrs. (57):   They (her parents) should have been stricter. My father should have put his foot down and I think that if he had done so and stopped his damn drinking, I would have been home at the age of 15 and not have gone out and got married.

Mrs. (14):   I was brought up, when I did something wrong, I was spanked. That was at the age of thirteen years old. As far as I can remember I was only hit once between the ages of 12 and 18. Of course, the reason I got hit was one day I deserved to get hit. I should have been hit a long time before I even got into that situation!

There are two major reasons given by parents for the use of violence on their children. First, violence is used instrumentally to teach and control. Second, violence is a form of discipline used to punish misbehavior.

*Teach and Control with Violence.* Violence is viewed by many parents as an effective tool for teaching or controlling children. Often, a parent will use force on a young child because the parent does not feel that he can communicate the message verbally.

Mrs. (7):    When she gets a little bit older, I don't want to have to spank her, I want to be able to just say, "you know, it's this way," or use a little bit of psychology on her without having to slap her. But right now she doesn't understand that much. I mean, you can't stand and explain really something in detail that she'll understand. So a slap sometimes. She understands when she gets a slap when she's done something wrong.

Mrs. (7) not only "communicates" with her child when she hits her, she believes that the child can understand being hit while she might not be able to comprehend a lecture or "a bit of psychology." Other mothers also feel that a swift slap or a spanking is a readily understandable technique for teaching a child not to do something or to control his behavior.

Mrs. (13):   My neighbor puts her child out and she sits right there with him. I don't see why you have to sit right there with your child. I mean, for a little while you can watch him, I mean all the time watch him. Like I put Manny out if I tell him to stay in the yard, he's going to stay in the yard. Because, you know, last summer every time he went out of the yard—I mean every time—I took a paddle and I spanked him. Because I saw a little girl get hit by a car and I don't figure that I am going to bring up my child to be hit by a car—so he won't leave the yard. Like sometimes, he'll say, "can I go play with the boys." But if a ball goes into the street Manny won't go after it. He don't know exactly—I mean he knows what a car is, but he don't know what it really means. Like I try to tell him to look both ways, well it doesn't mean much to him because he's too young. If you paddle his butt once or twice that's all it takes 'cause children aren't stupid.

In addition to use in teaching children the dangers of running out into the street, parents use slaps and spankings to instruct children not to touch expensive appointments in the home, stereo systems (a favorite "don't touch" item for fathers), television knobs, electric wires and plugs, and other taboo-to-touch objects.

Mrs. (74):   When she was younger we would try to teach her no if she was at the TV or the wires or something that would hurt her. She would get her wrist slapped.

Mrs. (60):   We've gathered stuff in our travels. Valuable stuff. The front room is full of stuff that you wouldn't want any child to grab and break and sometimes they might need a little paddle just to make them realize that they shouldn't touch.

In summary, parents use the slap, the spanking, and the strap to teach their children not to do things, to pay attention, and to control behavior. Force often is used as a resource when the parent cannot think of anything else that would be as effective. In training situations that are filled with frustration, a parent often will spank when no other method works.

> Mrs. (56):    Well, if I put him on the toilet and he won't do it and then I leave him there for an hour and then I take him off, and then ten minutes later he's done it in his pants. I mean that upsets me. What do I do? I spank him and let him know it's wrong then the time after that for a couple of days he's all right. And then he'll do it again. I think he avenges me. I don't know what it is. I think it's psychological—he's out to get me.

There is one pattern that emerges from the discussion of violence used to teach and control. Each parent who employs violence in this manner believes that force is necessary and cannot be avoided. However, the discussions also evidence the fact that the use of force is *not* unavoidable. Parents can attempt to reason with their children. They can sit and watch them to make sure they don't run into the street, and they can "child proof" their homes by removing valuable or dangerous objects from places that are accessible to children. One reason why parents fail to do this is because violence *is* so quick and efficient. Another important rationale is simply that striking a child in these situations is not considered violent: it *is* normative.

*Discipline.* There are countless incidents of children misbehaving and parents responding by hitting. It goes without saying that parents use physical violence to punish children for misbehavior and to inventory what children are hit for would not accomplish much because, as one mother puts it—"you name it, they do it, and I hit them for it."[3] There are two important facets of this type of violence that will be discussed. First, many of the parents interviewed stated that the thing that they could not stand in their child was back-talk, sassiness, or disrespect. Second, one interesting aspect of discipline violence is the notion of "an eye for an eye," where the parent feels the punishment ought to fit the crime.

When a child talks back to a parent, is "sassy," or in some manner disrespectful, the infraction almost uniformly is met by the parent striking the child. Parents repeatedly said that the thing that they hit their child the most for, or the only thing that they hit their child for, was "sassiness."

> Mr. (53): Well, my daughter, let's say my wife tells her to do something. She won't do it and she keeps kicking my wife or something, then I use the strap on her. I can't stand her to backtalk me. She backtalks me, I sometimes give her the strap, of course I don't give it to her as bad as I would if she starts kicking my wife or anything like that.

> Mr. (60): I spank her whenever she is disrespectful to my wife.

> Mrs. (80): Once, the oldest, she said "I hate you and nobody loves me and I hate you, Momma." I whacked her really good . . . I had a curtain rod and got her on her legs and her ass, too.

One of the classic cases was a father who punished his son for disrespect because his son was fresh in school.

> Mrs. (46): Sometimes I spank them and it doesn't do any good, I'll have my husband take a belt to them. My son, he was fresh in school and my husband got the teacher on the phone and she said he (the son) misbehaved. My husband took a belt and gave him a whack so the teacher could hear it.

Apparently, a child giving a parent backtalk establishes a powerful confrontation between child and parent. The child barks that he won't do something or that he hates the parent, and the parent uses physical force to assert his authority and power. Oftentimes, the confrontation is exacerbated by the parent's self-doubt concerning his or her role as a parent. One mother told how, when her daughter said she hated her and wanted to leave home, she just hit the daughter in the mouth—not because of the backtalk, but because the mother said that she felt that she was a failure if her daughter would say such a thing.

Another aspect of parental use of violence as an instrument of punishment is the ideology of "an eye for an eye." Even with very young children, parents are not hesitant to use force if they feel that the child's behavior warrants a spanking.

> Mrs. (75):    If he spits his food at me I slap his leg. No time to learn like the present—if he is old enough to do it, he's old enough to learn not to do it.

Mrs. (75) was speaking about her six-month-old baby. In other instances, parents state that the punishment should fit the crime. In the case of sassiness or backtalk, the punishment is a slap in the mouth:

> Mr. (42):    I believe that if they talk back with their mouth then that is where they should get it. If they break something I try to talk to find out why they broke it and try to make them understand why they shouldn't—by talking. If it is because they've been uptight and unable to settle down, I'd say a good spanking if they give you a ruckus.

Parents present a somewhat well-defined scheme for dealing out punishment—the punishment should match the crime. When physical violence is instigated by the child, the punishment is physical violence.

> Mrs. (69):    The only thing that I can remember that involved physically punishing them—they fight a lot. They are at an age where they're constantly killing each

other. And my husband would take them and make
them hit each other when they would get into a
fight—and then they didn't want to. They remember
him banging their heads together when they were
fighting.

One parent uses violence to punish violence even though
she is aware that this may teach the child to use violence
instrumentally.

Mrs. (75):    I can't tolerate unuseful teasing or something like
that. If one of the kids gets out of hand with their
hands and starts punching someone else—I suppose
you can't teach children about violence by using
violence—but that really turns me off and I give
them a good swat and up to their room.

The feature that characterizes the normal use of violence
to punish children is the elaborate calculus that parents
employ for deciding what type of behavior deserves what
type of punishment. There are both implicit and explicit
rules for using violence that parents develop in interaction
with their children that they expect their children to learn
and to adhere to. The child is expected to know that if he
does a certain thing he will receive a certain punishment. The
parent, on the other hand, tries desperately to follow these
rules and to punish the child consistently. Thus, an aspect of
normal violence between parent and child is the building of
common-sense understandings about rules of conduct and
rules of punishment.

*Neutralization of Violence.* The final section on normal
violence between parent and child discusses how parents
neutralize the use of physical force. Although parents argue
that children need to be and are hit when they deserve it,
parents still attempt to normalize the use of violence by
techniques of neutralization (Sykes and Matza, 1957). There
are a number of techniques used that downplay the actual
physical impact of the violence on the child and play up the

fact that spanking the child is supposed to "hurt" the parent more than the child.

One technique is to explain that it really doesn't hurt the child. One mother asserted that her husband used a belt because it only "stings."

Mrs. (34):   I think they've only got two spankings in their life from him and it was with the belt when he did it. I don't know why but to me it seems like it stings a little more than your hand would, and for that matter I've read in places where it says you shouldn't use your hand anyway. I can't explain it, but I just don't believe that you should use your hand.

Other parents justify hitting a child so long as "you don't leave marks."

Mrs. (27):   I used to use my hand—put them over my knee and give them a good swat. But then I got myself a little paddle—the ball broke off and I kept the paddle. Usually I just show them that. I don't believe in beating children or leaving marks.

Most parents we talked to stated that they would explain before, during, or after they hit their children why they were spanking them. The fact that the violence was explained to the child not only served to justify its use to the child but justified it to the parent.

One parent apparently overstepped the bounds of normal violence in that when she or her husband hit their son he would get quite black and blue. This, too, was neutralized.

Mrs. (13):   My husband spanks him and he bruises his butt and it's not because he is hitting him hard. I guess it's a different way of hitting him. If you, I guess, like with a paddle like what came up fast, I guess you draw their blood to the skin and it really makes you

> feel guilty. When I saw it I really felt like vomiting—
> I guess it's because you're hitting him the wrong
> way.

The fact that her husband hit her child hard enough to cause black and blue marks or make him bleed did not dissuade either of them from hitting the child. In fact, earlier Mrs. (13) was quoted as saying that a spanking is a good way to teach a child not to run into the street. Thus, because she approves of the use of violence she attempts to neutralize even severe beatings.

## Secondary Violence

One of the reasons why this chapter has examined parent-child violence, even though the main thrust of the research is on conjugal violence, is that it is often difficult to discuss parental violence apart from conjugal violence. Where these two intersect we find the type "Secondary Violence." Straus (1973: 115) suggests that when the use of violence to resolve a conflict is contrary to family norms it creates an additional conflict over violence. This "secondary conflict" tends to produce further violence. We have labeled this further violence as "secondary violence." The dynamics of secondary violence begin with parental employment of physical force on a child. While the parent who is using the violence believes it is legitimate and normal, the other parent, either because the spouse is "too" violent or because there were insufficient grounds for hitting the child, views this violence as illegitimate. This sets off a conflict between the partners that may lead to conjugal violence.

A major source of family conflict are these disagreements over how children should be raised—especially, what disciplinary actions should be taken. A number of wives complained that their husbands believe them to be too lenient.

> Mrs. (43):    Our major problem is that he's too strict and I am
> too lenient. Like if Wally took a straw and blew
> ashes from the ashtray—my husband said he was

going to get a good, big spanking for that. I dis-
agreed with him about it.

Spouses also feel that their partners may be too harsh on
the children. They either don't have a legitimate reason to
punish them or they punish them too severely.

Mrs. (54):     What bothers me is that I feel sometimes he is
               spanking her for nothing. He is taking things for
               granted—like he'll call her and she won't come. She
               is the type of child that if she's into something she
               won't hear a word you are saying. One time we had
               a fight over her because she said she had to go to the
               bathroom and he said she was using it for an excuse
               because she had already went to the bathroom. But
               I said, "look, you are not going to tell me when she
               has to go to the bathroom" . . . and we had a big
               fight over that. I felt he was wrong . . . in fact he
               spanked her that time.

The next step in secondary violence, once the partners
disagree over the use of force on the children, is for one
partner to intervene between the spouse and the child during
an incident of violence.

Mrs. (17):     But this was the type of person he was in the
               beginning. He was a perfectionist, in that he would
               go around door sills with his finger and if there
               would be any dust he would holler and you know—
               he would hit. . . . That's the kind of person he was,
               a perfectionist. When the babies were crying I re-
               member several incidents where he'd use his belt to
               whack them—and they were just a couple of months
               old and I'd go up and step in the way and then he'd
               start screaming at me.

From here the conflict often leads to conjugal violence. In
some instances, the aggressor turns on the wife who intervened and begins to hit her.

Mrs. (68):     He uses his hand . . . anywhere . . . but not now
               because they are really too big to hit.

Interviewer:   Do you ever intervene?

Mrs. (68):     Oh, yeah. I stick up for my kids. That was one of
               the instances where he sort of whacked me.

Secondary violence also may be initiated by the spouse
who is not hitting the child. Here the spouse uses violence to
turn the attention of the partner from the child to herself.

Mrs. (61):     I didn't object to him spanking them when they
               needed to be corrected or spanked. I wouldn't inter-
               fere then. But when he hit them violently or in
               anger, then I would interfere. Mostly, it was when
               he was after one of the kids. Our girl was home at
               the time. She was in school. We allowed her to take
               the car and she went to a dance. She was with
               another girl and she went to a dance. By the time
               she showed up home, which was about 1:00 a.m.,
               she was supposed to be here and she wasn't home
               until 2 . . . well the poor kid was panicky. My hus-
               band really raised the roof. My daughter was going
               upstairs to go to bed and he took his fist and hit her
               head against the side of the stairway, going up. He
               no sooner did that, than I hit him. That's the kind
               of knockdowns we had.

The sequence of secondary violence begins with what at
least one parent believes to be normal violence. The legitimacy of this act is questioned by the other spouse, which
leads to conflict over the legitimacy and normality of violence towards children. Occasionally, the parent who argues
against the unreasonable use of violence on the children will
intervene. The intervention may be in the form of a violent
attack against the spouse, or it may be verbal intervention, or
getting between the aggressor and child. This intervention

may lead to the aggressor turning from the child to the spouse.

*Threats*

*"This is what will happen to you if you're not careful!"* There is a type of violence that is not violent at all—that is, threats of violence. Komarovsky (1967: 227) labeled the threat of violence as a source of masculine power. We found numerous incidents of husbands punching holes in walls, breaking down doors, firing guns, and breaking dishes—all of which were designed to demonstrate to the wife what could happen to her if she got out of line. One 28-year-old wife cited how her husband would break things.

> Mrs. (75): A lot of times he would go out at night and he wouldn't come home until late. One time I locked the door and he broke the window. He got mad and broke things—not at me. One time he punched the wall and put a hole in it.

In addition to using the demonstration of violence as a threat, husbands also might threaten to kill themselves or to hit family members. Mrs. (6), who had been beaten by her husband when first married, discussed how he threatened further violence.

> Mrs. (6): He had an awful temper and he'd threaten to put his fist through the wall, or threaten to kill himself, or all kinds of threats.

The gun is often a rather terrifying device used by husbands to threaten violence. A divorced wife recalls how her husband used to get angry and start shooting up the house.

> Mrs. (48): He had a violent temper, in fact I've got bullet holes at the old house in the walls to prove it. He also put his fist through the walls a couple of times. One night he went into the bedroom and the next thing I knew the gun went off and there was a bullet hole

in the wall, and he slammed the gun down and out
the house he went.

The use of a gun to threaten a spouse with violence is not
restricted to actually firing the gun.

Mrs. (17):     He threatened me with the gun. I don't know where
               he had the gun hidden. I didn't want him to keep it
               in sight because of the kids. But at night he'd put
               the bullets on my bureau and then left the gun in
               his drawer.

Although 33% of the wives in this study used physical
violence at least once, we found no incidents of a wife
threatening her husband with violence. Most wives use other
resources such as withholding sexual favors (as was found by
Komarovsky, 1967: 227), threatening to call the police, to
take the children away, or to go away themselves. Thus,
violent threats are typically used by the husband to intimi-
date or coerce deference from the wife.

## Volcanic Violence

Volcanic violence represents a type of violence that is
accounted for neither with the explanation that it was used
to achieve a desired end, nor with any attempt to neutralize
or legitimize the act. Volcanic violence occurs when the
offender has reached the end of the line—has run out of
patience as the result of externally caused stress such as
losing a job, frustration at being unable to communicate with
his spouse, or victim-induced frustration (where the victim
badgers the offender until he can take no more). Volcanic
violence is illegitimate violence that is explained as arising out
of the buildup of stress and frustration. The stress builds to
the point where the offender "erupts" into violence.

In some cases, the frustration comes from sources external
to the family. The husband of Mrs. (48) erupted into the
shooting incident mentioned in the previous section after his
driver's license was suspended. This meant that he would

have to lose his job as a delivery man. When frustration reaches an intolerable level, the conclusion is often violence, as it is in the family of Mrs. (16).

> Mrs. (16):  He's hit me before—several times. It gets to the point he ahhh—I guess he gets frustrated. I don't know why, it's upsetting even for the children to see him like that.

Occasionally, stress and frustration result from family interaction.

> Mrs. (10):  Well, he just got very very violently mad at me because it was so ridiculous—it was a ridiculous thing, I know. It was during a big snow storm we had and the children and I worked for 1½ hours on a Friday night to clear out the driveway to the street so he could get his car in. And the next morning he didn't want to get up and shovel out my car. He said my son Billy and I could do it. And Billy can't even shovel. And so we went out there and tried to do it and it was impossible. Billy and I would just take two shovelfuls and then die in the snow. So I came in, you know, and asked him if he wouldn't please help me. I said, "My God, Tom, we worked for an hour and a half clearing the driveway for you and you can't even turn and help me." Well he was too busy reading his papers and didn't want to be bothered and he was just tired. And I guess I pushed him to the point where I bitched at him for not helping me, and that he was driven to the point where he got up, threw his papers down and came at me. He called me very bad names and from here to there he sent me with an open hand. And my right eye hemorrhaged completely.

This account reveals that there are two types of victim-precipitated violence: where the victim feels that she deserved to be hit, this is normal violence; and where the victim is not willing to justify the act, this is illegitimate, volcanic violence.

Volcanic violence usually results in the more severe incidents of family violence. Husbands who hit wives, wives who hit husbands, and parents who hit children as a result of reaching the end of their patience all report that these were the most extensive episodes of violence in their families. One young wife lost control of herself and started slapping and choking her youngest daughter. A 23-year-old wife told of how her previous husband beat her so badly that she blacked out.

Some volcanic violence occurs when one spouse is unable to communicate with the other in the course of an argument. Both husbands and wives resort to violence under the pressure and frustration of a family quarrel that they are unable to compete in.

> Mrs. (52):  He would just yell and yell—not really yell, just talk loudly. And I couldn't say anything because he kept talking. So I'd swing.

A number of wives reported that they erupted into violence after they stayed home alone for a long period of time. The isolation bred frustration, which led to violence.

> Mrs. (55):  He made me so mad . . . I spent most of my time alone . . . the first years I spent most of my time alone, and after that I moved and was still home alone. I spent all that time by myself and sometimes the kids would get on my nerves . . . so when I got mad I hit him.

Mothers, whether they are home or work all day, are delegated the role of raising the children and are the members of the family who experience the greatest frustrations in childrearing. Many mothers who are home all day or who have a limited time to govern their children because they work will hit their children when they reach the end of their patience. A 40-year-old widow discussed how hard it is to care for children without the help of her husband.

Mrs. (18): Well, Lori is my main problem. She'll stomp her feet and she keeps running off at the mouth sassing— "I'm not going to do this and I have to do everything." I keep telling her to keep quiet—"Shut up while you're ahead of the game." This will go on for days before I strike out at her. And finally, when I get to the point where I can't take no more, I spank her. She knows she's been spanked when I get through with her. I don't like to hit her because I don't stop.

The eruption of conjugal violence occurs with equal frequency among both husbands and wives. In terms of parent-child violence, it is the mother who usually explodes into violence when she runs out of patience. The accounts of volcanic violence in no way try to justify the incidents—the violence is expressive and illegitimate in the eyes of the family members.

## Alcohol-Related Violence

A number of studies of interpersonal violence report a high association between violence and alcohol (Gillen, 1946; Guttmacher, 1960; Wolfgang, 1958). Alcohol is viewed as acting as a "super-ego solvent" that releases aggression and violence. We found the same high association between alcohol and violence in the 80 families. One important feature of the finding was that alcohol-related violence is almost exclusively *male violence.* In only one family did the wife become violent towards her husband and children when she was drinking.

The respondents who discussed violent incidents that occurred while they or their spouse were drinking or drunk explained that the cause of the violence was the alcohol. They almost invariably explained that when the spouse was sober, he was neither violent nor abusive. A 45-year-old widow commented that her late husband had been two different men, one sober and pleasant, the other drunk and evil.

Mrs. (19):   When he was sober he was very, very nice, but when he was drunk, he was terribly irrational. I think I can't begin to tell you what fear is, honey . . . he was a big man, you know and he was very irrational, very ugly like what do you say—"Mr. Hyde and Dr. Jekyll." This is the type of man he was when he was . . . that was what drinking would do to him and he would have to be drunk to react the way he did because he wouldn't do it when he was sober. He would do it when he was drunk so most of his life he was drunk.

Mrs. (51), a waitress, told how her husband only hit her when he was drinking.

Mrs. (51):   He hit me many times. But at first, like I say, it was only when he was drinking . . . he wouldn't ever slap me when he was sober no matter how mad he got.

The respondents' accounts of violent behavior when their spouse was drinking confirms the conventional wisdom that alcohol serves as a disinhibitory agent that releases violent impulses. We will return to this assumption and discuss how the dynamics of alcohol-related violence argue against this conventional wisdom in the next chapter when the violent situation is examined.

### Protective-Reaction Violence

The next type of family violence takes its name from the account of the United States government of the heavy bombing of Cambodia and Vietnam in the late sixties and early seventies. The rationale for the bombing was that a "protective-reaction strike" was devised to "hit the enemy before he hits us" and to cripple the enemy's capacity to fight. Or, a "protective-reaction strike" could be a bombing raid carried out in retaliation for an enemy attack, such as the Offensive of 1968. There is a striking similarity between these justifications of national violence and accounts of certain family violence.

Protective-reaction violence, in contrast to alcohol-related violence, which is usually male violence, is female violence. Wives are the family members who initiate protective-reaction strikes against their husbands. In the first instance of protective-reaction violence, the wife commences a preemptive attack because she fears that her husband is getting ready to hit her.

> Mrs. (13):  Last week—I don't know if he was going to hit me—I think he was. He was trying to show me that he was angry and then . . . Yea, I showed him I was angry because I am pregnant and if he ever hit me, I think I'd hurt him or do something. Leave him or something. Anyway, he was laying down and I was sitting next to him, and we were talking, and he got mad, and he got up, and he come right up to my face and he . . . and I went like this and I punched him. It wasn't out of anger. It was out of fear. I was afraid that he was going to hit me . . . it was out of fright, he scared me.

Other incidents of protective-reaction violence occur *after* the husband has initiated the attack. If the wife believes her husband is wrong, she may decide to retaliate or to hit back in self-defense. Mrs. (51), whose husband hits her when drunk, hits back because she feels that he is no match for her when he's drunk.

> Mrs. (51):  Well, he was wrong, right? So I got angry, too. You get a slap out of nowhere—I knew I was stronger than him, when he was drunk that is, so I gave him a

> good shove and a kick—whatever I could kick—I
> didn't aim. And then he'd end up on the floor and
> I'd beat the daylights out of him.

Not many wives are ready or willing to take on their
husbands in hand-to-hand combat. Retaliatory violence frequently escalates the conflict because the wives feel that they
are in need of weapons when they hit back. When this
happens, wives often will strike their husbands with heavy
objects or go after them with knives.

Mrs. (69):    When he hit me I would retaliate. Maybe a woman
doesn't have the strength to hold her own, but I
sure want to go down trying . . . I hit him back . . . I
am more liable to pick up something than hit him
with my fist.

Mrs. (80):    After he hit me, I went after him with a knife and
put him in the hospital.

The wives who respond to violence with more extensive
violence justify this because they feel that when they hit
back they are likely to be hit harder by their husbands; thus,
Mrs. (80) stabs her husband and Mrs. (69) hits her husband
with a lamp so that they will incapacitate them and stave off
a severe beating.

## One-Way Violence

There are wives who, when their husbands physically
assault them, do not hit back. This type of violence, one-way
violence, also can be considered a subtype of volcanic,
alcohol-related violence. The constraints that operate on a
wife to prevent her from hitting back are usually pragmatic.
Wives who do not fight back do not because they are afraid
that if they do, they will be hit even harder. Two women
recall how they reacted when their husbands beat them.

Mrs. (3):    My husband (former husband) beat me and pushed
me down the stairs. I would just sit alone and cry

when he beat me up—and he did quite often. I never
called the police or hit him back because if I did
that he would have beat the shit out of me.

Mrs. (27):     It was rather tense at times, but I never would dare
to hit him. . . . I'd get it right back, I'm sure.

Fear of being hit was not the only factor operating on
wives who were hit by their husbands. Mrs. (14) said that she
would have liked to hit her husband, but somehow it just
isn't right for a woman to hit.

Mrs. (14):     I've wanted to slap him right on the side of the head
or throw something at him. Like I said, I think for a
man and woman are fighting, like, if the woman—
well, a man can get over anger—he can go punch a
wall or something and people won't think he's nuts
or something, or he can get in his car and wheel off,
or go and get drunk, or go get in a street fight. But a
woman, she can't do nothing, you know, she's
there, she's mad and she can't hit him. I think it's a
good idea if women can throw things and I mean
not expensive things that can break up things—like
throw a plate or something across the room.

What Mrs. (14) seems to be saying is that not only can a
man hit his wife when he gets mad, there are a number of
alternatives available by which he can blow off steam—
alternatives that are legitimate and even normative in certain
subcultures. But the wife, the culturally passive female, just
must steam—or throw plates—she is not "allowed" to get into
street fights or hit back at her husband.

Although there is a general belief on the part of the wives
who do not hit back that this will diminish the conflict and
lessen the chances of their being hit further, there are indications that the effect of not hitting back works in the reverse—
that is, an individual who does not hit back is more likely to
be hit repeatedly. Kaplan (1972: 610) comments that aggression is more likely if the other person (the victim) is per-

ceived of as unwilling or unable to retaliate. Indeed, our respondents who did not fight back were still the recipients of repetitive aggression from their husbands. On the other hand, the respondents who *did* fight back were also hit often, so we are left with no real answer as to what posture by the victim reduces the occurrence of beatings.

### Sex-Related Violence: Jealousy

Earlier, during the discussion of normal violence, violence that accompanied suspected cheating on the part of one of the spouses was examined and the victim stated that she had "deserved to be hit." There are, however, other sex-related incidents of violence where the accompanying violence is not defined as legitimate.

Sex-related violence, as discussed here, stems from jealousy. Spouses often will hit each other in the course of jealous arguments over suspected cheating, running around, or flirtation in nonfamily social settings. Whitehurst (1971: 1974) has discussed the issue of violence potential in extramarital sexual responses and the case of violently jealous husbands. Extramarital sexual relations or flirtations violate the basic and traditional norms of fidelity in families. These infractions often evoke violent responses in males and females whose socialization experiences have taught them to use violence in such situations.

Typically, sex-related violence is accompanied by a lengthy interrogation of the partner who is suspected of cheating. Often, there is quite concrete evidence available for the jealous partner to use to commence the interrogation. Mrs. (46), the wife of a plumber, was having marital problems and discusses how a violent confrontation grew out of one incident of suspected cheating.

> Mrs. (46):  I was getting ready to leave him. I didn't talk to him or bother with him. I knew this friend—in fact he was just divorced. He was a good school chum of my husband's and he called me up one day to ask me how I was. He knew about it (the fight with her

husband) because we met at his place on New Year's. He took a girlfriend because he was just divorced. We went to dinner and we met him at the lounge—so he had seen how my husband acted. He called me up a few days later. He said, "I'm surprised at the way your husband acted." So I told him that I was thinking of leaving my husband. So he said, "Well, I always go down to the Melnack Lounge. If you're lonesome come on down." So that night I went out to get my daughter some clothes and I snuck out. Why should I sit home and brood all night? That was how I figured it, it was the end anyway. So I went down to the Melnack and we were dancing and he bought me a few drinks. When I got home, my husband was up—of course, I was all dressed up. I had a dress on and everything. And he said, "Where were you?" And I said, "What difference does it make? You don't care about me anyway." He slapped me and took his hand and whacked me and he wouldn't let me sleep. He said, "You are not going to bed until you tell me where you've been!" So at first, I wouldn't tell him. . . . He slapped me again because I had gone out. "You've been running around!" he said. So finally I had to tell him.

From a husband's point of view, continued lying about cheating is just too much to take.

Mr. (74):     She was going out with other guys. I tried to discuss the problem and she denied the whole thing. After a while I got to her. In that case . . . she kept lying about it . . . so you get tired of this. One night coming home from going out . . . something happened, she kept denying the thing. I just grabbed her and threw her on the lawn. I don't remember what happened then. I had a few drinks anyway.

Sometimes, the interrogations and the violence that follows, take on the aura of "Gestapo Violence." Mrs. (69),

who had been beaten quite often by her husband, tells of
lengthy sessions of the "Third Degree" followed by beatings.

> Mrs. (69):  He would come in and harp on a certain thing. And
> he would keep it up until finally you would admit
> to anything in the world to get him to shut up. He
> would keep it up for 5 hours and not let me sleep. I
> would say, "Yes! Yes! I did, are you glad?" . . . and
> then he would beat me.

Sex-related violence is one of the types of violence where
husbands and wives are equally aggressive. A retired cook,
Mr. (22) was verbally and physically attacked by his jealous
wife.

> Mr. (22):  She's always been a very jealous woman. I don't
> know why, there's no woman that would run after
> me. I'm always working anyway. She always had it
> in her mind that I was going out with someone. . . .
> Many times she's thrown things at me. . . . Once she
> hit me with a radio—of course I ducked. She threw
> dishes.

One interesting aspect of sex-related violence, an aspect
that places it on the border of legitimate and illegitimate
violence, is the reaction of victims who have been hit after
they accused their spouses of cheating. Here the accuser is
the victim, not the offender. But the accuser views the
violence as an indication that the accusation is true, and that
their spouse *was* cheating. The victim in these cases looks at
the violence as proof positive of infidelity; and thus, is not
completely upset about being hit. One husband reports an
incident with his former wife where the accusations led to
him being hit.

> Mr. (64):  We had a couple of fights about a friend of mine. I
> worked nights, and he was stopping by to keep her
> company. I told him to keep the Christ away from

my house, and she said that I didn't trust her. One time she hit me ... she took a glass tray with a sterling center post and conked me with that while I wasn't looking—she was very violent. She hits me over this thing with this guy. She took it as a direct thing. It turned out to be true, she was having an affair with this guy. It's a miracle that I didn't go out because she really put a hell of a dent in my head. She came back and said she was sorry, but by then I was thinking that I must have hit on the truth.

## A TYPOLOGY OF FAMILY VIOLENCE

The development of types of intrafamily violence that emerged from the interviews with the 80 families reveals that family violence is far from a unitary phenomenon. The types of violence and meanings of violence that have been discussed evidence at least three major dimensions of physical violence. The first two dimensions have been discussed by Straus and his associates (Steinmetz and Straus, 1973; Owens and Straus, 1973; and Straus, Gelles, and Steinmetz, 1973) in discussions of family violence. These two dimensions are: (1) Whether the use of physical force is an end in itself—"expressive" violence; or whether physical violence, restraint, and pain are intended as a means of inducing another person to carry out some act or alter his behavior—"instrumental" violence. (2) Whether the violence under consideration is required, authorized, or approved under the rules of society, subculture, or social group of the actor—"legitimate" violence; or whether it is prohibited or deprecated by the society or group—"illegitimate" violence. To these two dimensions, the data on violence suggest the addition of a third dimension—the role of the victim. Victims of physical violence can contribute more or less to their own victimization. In some instances, they directly contribute through either actions defined as illegitimate by the offender or through provoking their antagonist—"victim-precipitated violence"; or the victim can play little or no active part in the violence and simply be the available, accessible, or in some way "proper" target for the violence—"not-victim-precipitated violence." In terms of this dimension, it is difficult to actually dichotomize the two because, in reality, the level of precipitation may be a continuum rather than just an "either, or" determination. This, however, also applies to the other two dimensions. The main purpose of including victim precipitation in the typology is because it illustrates the dynamics of violence and the role the victim plays in different types of violent occurrences.

The combination of these three dimensions of violence produces an eight-fold typology of violence (2 x 2 x 2). (See Figure 1). There are no entrees into the eight cells because the categorization of incidents of intrafamily violence depends on whose norms and whose perspective one takes when evaluating the violent episodes. There are a variety of perspectives that can be utilized.

|  | EXPRESSIVE | | INSTRUMENTAL | |
|  | Victim-Precipitated | Not-Victim-Precipitated | Victim-Precipitated | Not-Victim-Precipitated |
| --- | --- | --- | --- | --- |
| **LEGITIMATE** | 1 | 2 | 3 | 4 |
| **ILLEGITIMATE** | 5 | 6 | 7 | 8 |

Figure 1. A TYPOLOGY OF FAMILY VIOLENCE

## The "Offender"

One way of determining whether hitting a family member is expressive or instrumental, legitimate or illegitimate, victim-precipitated or not, is to rely on the account or definition of the situation of the individual who used the force. This perspective largely would depend on how the hitter "accounted for" (Lyman and Scott, 1970; Komarovsky, 1940) the act of hitting. Often, husbands who hit their wives will say that they simply lost control of themselves or could not control their tempers. In these cases, the violence would be classified as expressive. If the attacker says that he hit the victim to "bring him to his senses," or "to teach her a lesson," or "they needed to be hit," then the violence would be considered instrumental. Similarly, if the offender describes the incident in such a way as to display feelings of committing a deviant act, then the hitting or the attack would be classified as illegitimate. If the actor feels that the hitting of a family member was justified, then it would be a legitimate mode of violence from his perspective.

## The "Victim"

It is all well and good that the offender may feel that hitting the victim was justified or that the violence was used to teach a lesson, but what of the victim's feelings about being hit? The incidents of violence also may be classified on the basis of his definition of the situation. If the victim's response to the violence was "thanks, I needed that," then from his perspective the violence was legitimate. On the other hand, the victim may feel that being slapped across the face was completely unwarranted.

## Joint Perspective

A third approach would be a conjoint definition of the situation. Here the perspectives of both actors (offender and victim) are taken into account in determining what type of violence took place. Faulkner (1971) bases his discussion of violence in professional hockey on interviews with a number of players who are sometimes offenders, sometimes victims of attacks. His discussion seems to indicate that, while violence in hockey is often expressive, it is occupationally necessary and a legitimate form of expression. This conclusion is not drawn solely from talking with aggressive hockey players, but also by interviewing hockey players who are, more often than not, on the receiving end of violence.

Another joint perspective may take into consideration the entire family's view of the violence. Here the collective familial definition of the situation is used to type incidents of violence. A critical aspect of this perspective would be the family's collective and shared meanings (Hess and Handel, 1959) concerning types and usage of violence.

## Agents of Control

A fourth alternative is to use the perspective of agents of control in classifying violence. Here the classification is based on the views of agents of control (such as the police, the courts, or other public officials) as to what constitutes expressive or instrumental; legitimate or illegitimate violence. In terms of child abuse, the decision as to whether a child is actually abused (illegitimate violence) is largely based on a doctor's referral of the case to the courts or to the police. Thus, even though the parents may deny that any abuse or illegitimate violence took place—which is often the case in incidents of child abuse (Kempe, 1962)—the incident may be viewed as illegitimate by an agent of control. Similarly, a policeman's discretion separates routine family brawls from criminal assault in that he can decide to either arrest an assailant, or allow him to remain at home.

## The Investigator

The final perspective that may be utilized is that of the investigator or researcher. He can decide on the basis of his analysis of the interview protocols whether an attack was instrumental or expressive in intent. This is the procedure used in Bales "Interaction Process Analysis" (1950) to code behavior in small group laboratory experiments, where the researcher rather than the actor codes behavior into the different categories (except that the actual behavior is not observed in research on family violence).

The investigator's ability to use a variety of criteria by which to code violence further enlarges the number of possible ways in which violence may be typed. For instance, the investigator may use legal criteria of assault in coding for legitimacy and illegitimacy of violence, or he may use his own personal standards of appropriate forms of intrafamilial behavior.

It is obvious that the typing of violence, for the most part, will depend on which of the five different perspectives are used. Furthermore, it should not be surprising that each perspective is quite likely to be different from the others—what the offender sees as legitimate the victim may not; what the researcher finds appalling, the family may find normal and stable. In developing the types of violence in the previous section, we used a combination of the investigator's perspective and the subjective definitions of the situation given by the respondents—usually the victim in conjugal violence and the offender in parental violence. Whose definition of the situation to use in any specific investigation or analysis depends on the purpose of the analysis. Thus, a crucial decision that must be made in utilizing or filling in the cells of the typology is which perspective or combination of perspectives will be employed.

The major contribution of the eight-fold typology of violence is that it presents family violence as a multifaceted phenomenon. Where wife beating is commonly viewed as one type of deviant behavior, the use of the typology reveals that some wife beating may be viewed as normal, legitimate, instrumental violence by the participants where the wife caused or deserved to be hit. On the other hand, a husband may attack the wife without her provoking the attack and be venting his anger in expressive-illegitimate violence. Furthermore, wife beating also may be related to sex or alcohol. Child abuse, child battering, or child beating also can be examined using the types of violence and the typology. In some instances, child abuse may be normal violence where a chance factor led to the child being injured. One of the respondent's normal punishment of his son led to unintentional harm.

Mrs. (43):    Once, well, he slapped Alan and he was aiming for Alan's behind and Alan is a wiggler, so Alan turned

> around and got it right in the eye . . . his eye started
> turning black and blue here. That was a year ago . . .
> since then my husband has been more careful . . .
> he's a big man, very strong.

Had Mrs. (43) brought her son to a hospital for treatment, and the son had said his father hit him, in accordance with state law, the doctor might have reported the family as abusive parents.

Much child abuse occurs as volcanic violence where the victim somehow precipitated the attack. The child abuse literature (Gelles, 1973) reports many cases of abusive parents losing control when they could not restrain the child, toilet train him, or when the child demanded more attention than the parent(s) would give. Other cases of child abuse also fall into the instrumental/illegitimate/not-victim-precipitated category.

The purpose of presenting the typology has been two-fold. First, the types of family violence discussed in this chapter have been developed from interviews with 80 families, and may not be exhaustive. Therefore, the typology was devised to provide a framework for developing other types of family violence based on additional data. Second, the typology, rather than being an end in itself, provides an analytic tool by which to examine the range and variety of incidents of intrafamily violence.

## NOTES

1. It again must be pointed out that in the selection of the neighbors, no attempt was made to make this population representative of any general population. Thus, great care must be taken in generalizing the incidence of violence in these families to any population of families. The frequency of conjugal violence in these families may be inflated because of the fact that they are neighbors of families who were selected for the study because of the high possibility of violent incidents. Thus, factors such as "contagion," subculture of violence (Wolfgang and Ferracuti, 1967), or even social structure of violence (Coser,

1967) may contribute to a higher incidence of violence than in a randomly selected population of families. Of course, on the other hand, the incidence of violence in the neighbor families may be reduced by the fact that if they have been exposed to incidents of violence next door, this may set a boundary or a threshhold of violence lower than in families without violent neighbors.

2. When a respondent reported that they "fooled around" and "wrestled" or "play fought" with their spouse, this was *not* recorded as an incident of violence. Reports of "accidental" hitting or pushing *were* recorded as violence if the respondent reported that the "accident" was a result of the spouse not knowing his own strength. However, if the incident *was* accidental, such as a husband's hand slipping while opening a jar and hitting the wife, then this was not recorded as a violent incident.

3. Because parent-child violence is not the dominant focus of this research I have decided not to pursue the use of force to punish children in this section. However, this does not mean that this is an unimportant issue. One possible avenue for investigation is to examine how different ethnic, age, and socioeconomic groups punish children and whether or not the types of misbehavior for which children are hit vary across groups.

*Chapter 3*

# NO PLACE TO GO: THE VIOLENT SITUATION

One reason why we know so little about intrafamily violence is that the typical locale of the incidents is the home, during times of the day when no one except family members are present. Because of this, family violence takes on a very special character, which differentiates it from public occurrences of violence.

When violence occurs in public there are often bystanders or "seconds" present to intervene and either break up the fight or aid one of the participants. Violence in the home is a private affair with no bystanders and frequently no seconds available to help out one of the combatants. If violence occurs in a public setting like a tavern or a street corner, someone may call the police before or during the incident to break up the altercation. In violence between family members, typically the police are called by a family member only after the damage has been done (although sometimes a neighbor will call the police). If a violent confrontation is brewing in public, one or both of the participants may leave the scene by simply walking out of the bar or running down the street. When violence takes place in the home, there is often no place to go, and to leave the scene means leaving one's possessions, one's children, and one's home territory. Thus, when violence occurs between family members, there are few people who the participants can turn to for help and often no place to which the victim or offender can retreat.

This chapter analyzes conjugal violence by focusing on components of the violent situation: the location of the incident; the time of day, the day of the week, the time of year; and the presence or absence of other people.[1] The other component of the violent situation that is analyzed in this chapter is the previously cited high association between alcohol and violence. In this section, the "conventional wisdom" about alcohol functioning as a disinhibitory agent that releases aggression is challenged. Instead of positing that alcohol is a causal agent in violent situations, we examine the use of alcohol as it functions as a means for family members to disavow the deviance (Davis, 1961; McCaghy, 1968) of violence, and as a "time out" mechanism (MacAndrew and Edgerton, 1969) that gives the attacker the excuse that "I didn't know what I was doing."

The data used to examine the violent situation were derived from interviews with the 44 families who discussed at least one violent incident. Because of the informal interviewing technique, and because not all the respondents could remember the exact details of each violent situation, there are varying numbers of respondents who report information about the different aspects of the violent situation. Most of the respondents were able to remember whether alcohol was involved in the incident, many could remember in what room violence occurred. More than half the respondents were able to cite the time of day but few could remember the day of the week, or time of the year when violence occurred.

## VIOLENCE IN THE HOME: SPATIAL LOCATION

Violence between family members, whether it is pushing, shoving, beating, or homicide, usually takes place in the

home. Of the 30 respondents who discussed the spatial location of violence, all mentioned violence in the home and only
four mentioned incidents where violence occurred outside
the home. Wolfgang's study of criminal homicide found that
112 of 136 homicides (82%) where the offender and victim
were members of the same family occurred in the home
(1958: 378). Pokorny (1965) states that 71.9% of the
husband-wife homicides took place in the home. Pittman and
Handy's study of assault revealed a similar pattern where,
when the relation of the offender to victim was kin, then the
act was likely to be indoors—42 of 47 assaults (89%) between
members of the same family occurred in the combatants'
residence (1964: 465).

The respondents' discussion of the violent situation revealed that the typical location of family violence was the
kitchen (Table 7). The bedroom and living room are the next
most likely scenes of violence. Some respondents are unable
to pinpoint exact locations because their battles begin in one

### TABLE 7
### SPATIAL LOCATIONS OF CONJUGAL VIOLENCE
### MENTIONED BY RESPONDENTS

| PLACE | Percent Respondents Mentioning Location (N=30) |
| --- | --- |
| Kitchen | 63 |
| Bedroom | 27 |
| Living Room | 27 |
| TV Room | 3 |
| Dining Room | 3 |
| Hall | 7 |
| Front Steps | 3 |
| All Over House | 17 |
| Out of House (movie, bar, street, and so on) | 7 |
| Car | 7 |

room and progress throughout the house. The *only* room in the house where there was *no violence* was the bathroom!

The data on family violence are somewhat different from those on homicide. Homicide research finds that the bedroom is the deadliest room in the house (Pokorny, 1965; Wolfgang, 1958). Wolfgang (1958: 125) reports that 20% of all victims of criminal homicide were killed in the bedroom and that the bedroom is the room where a female is most likely to be killed (35% of female victims in the Wolfgang study were killed in the bedroom). The next most likely place where family homicides occur is the kitchen (Wolfgang, 1958: 213). Women are the usual offenders in the kitchen— 29% of the female offenders killed in this room (Wolfgang, 1958: 126). Pokorny's data (1965) showed that the living room or dining room ranked ahead of the kitchen.

Perhaps the reason for the difference in location between this study and previous studies has something to do with the difference in the type of violence: nonlethal violence in the case of the present study as compared to lethal violence in the studies reviewed.

### The Spatial Dynamics of Family Violence

Why is the home or apartment the arena of family combat, and why are certain spatial locations in the home frequently battlegrounds? To answer these questions requires some tentative analysis of the dynamics of family violence.

The home or apartment seems to be the locale of family violence for two major reasons. First, and obviously, it is here where the majority of family life and family interaction takes place. Second, the home is the "backstage" region (Goffman, 1959: 112) of family behavior. Protected by the privacy of one's own walls there is no need to maintain the presentation of family life as harmonious, loving, and conflict-free. All 80 respondents spoke of the home as a sort of refuge where they could retreat in order to avoid getting involved in other people's problems and a place where they could fight out their own differences in private.

Because the house or apartment is a family's home territory, it is where most of the family's life and identity is
grounded. Clothes, furniture, checkbooks, money, and other
worldly possessions are stored in the home. In addition, this
is where the children are brought up. Consequently, the
home or apartment is a place where individuals often flee *to*
under stress rather than flee *from*. Because it is difficult to
suddenly pick up and leave all of one's possessions, including
one's children, and because the house is home territory for
*both* combatants in family quarrels, there is great difficulty
in leaving the scene when conflict is festering. A number of
respondents discussed how, when they got mad, they simply
bolted out of the house and went for a drive, or to a tavern,
or to their mother's. But even though they were temporarily
able to leave the scene, they still eventually returned to their
own residence.

Within the home, the kitchen is the typical scene of
nonlethal family violence. The kitchen, because it is one of
the few rooms in the house where all family members rou-
tinely congregate for a period of time, is the place where
most total family interaction takes place (father, mother, *and*
children). The kitchen is where family news is exchanged
over dinner, children are asked and report what happened at
school, the wife relives her day, and the husband may discuss
what happened at work (Bossard and Boll, 1966: 142). The
potential for family arguments and family conflict is quite
high here considering that family members are somewhat
constrained to remain in the kitchen until dinner is complete,
and that conflict-prone topics such as children's behavior
during the day and financial matters are frequently discussed
over dinner. Mrs. (73) discusses why most of her family's
arguments took place in the kitchen:

Mrs. (73):     I guess the worst room in the house is the dinner
               table. I think it is terrible. A man comes home to
               eat his dinner and somebody's, I don't mean every
               night, but if anything . . . see, I'm alone every day,

> all day, and if there's something that might be
> worrying me, I can't quote anything off hand, it
> builds up in me all day. All I got to do is think. And
> by the time he gets home I'm just ready to pop off
> and it's typically at the dinner table.

The kitchen, because it is a focal point of family activity,
becomes the prime setting for conflict and whatever violence
might follow. Even during noneating time, the kitchen remains a high activity room.

> Mrs. (68):    Most of the incidents took place when he was drink-
>               ing . . . they took place in the kitchen, the kitchen
>               has more activity than any room in the house.

The second most likely room for violence is the living
room. The living room is a high violence location for similar
reasons to the kitchen. Here much family activity goes on,
and the television is usually located in the living room. The
television, in fact, may set off family violence. One wife
talked about her husband hitting her because she got in the
way of the television.

> Mrs. (59):    Once, when I was pregnant. I wanted to talk with
>               him about something. He had come home from
>               work. I don't remember what it was. He had the TV
>               on and he didn't want to listen to me. We had a big
>               fight. He pushed me. He must have wanted to push
>               me out of the way. I wouldn't move so he pushed
>               me.

Another wife, when she gets mad at her husband, sometimes
throws the television to get his attention.

The room in the house where most homicides occur and
where much nonlethal violence also takes place is the bedroom. The bedroom is the scene of conjugal battles for
reasons different from those for the other rooms. Much of
the conflict that occurs in this room revolves around sex and

intimacy. Arguments about a wife being "frigid" or a husband *not* being sexually aggressive enough were discussed by respondents who related incidents of bedroom-based physical violence. Another factor that leads to violence in the bedroom is that this is a difficult place to escape from. While a husband or wife may bolt from the dinner table, or out of the living room and out of the house, to do this from the bedroom is quite difficult considering the time required to get dressed and the fact that, at bedtime, where does one run to out of the house?

There is one room in the home where we heard no reports of violent incidents taking place—the bathroom. The bathroom is truly the demilitarized zone of the home. In addition, the bathroom is a room that almost always has a lock on the door. If no other room in the house has a lock, the bathroom still does. The neutral zone nature of the bathroom is preserved by its being a room where little conflict takes place. Perhaps, the bathroom serves as a refuge for family members to hide in to avoid violence.

## TIME AND VIOLENCE

### Time of Day

The families reported that the time of day when they were most likely to engage in physical combat was in the evening—from after dinner (8:00 PM) until bedtime (11:30 PM). The next most likely time was during or around dinner time (5:00 PM to 8:00 PM). Late evening, a time period that runs from bedtime until morning, comprises the third most violence-prone hours for conjugal combat (Table 8).

Our data are quite similar to the discussions of temporal patterns of criminal homicide. Wolfgang found that 50% of all criminal homicides occur between 8:00 PM and 2:00 AM (1958: 108). Fifty-five percent of our respondents mentioned incidents of violence occurring in this time frame. The second deadliest time of the day was from 2:00 PM until

8:00 PM (Wolfgang, 1958: 108). The families interviewed reported that this was a high violence time of day in their families. Similar patterns also were found in Pokorny's study of homicide (1965).

TABLE 8
## TIME OF DAY OF CONJUGAL VIOLENCE
## MENTIONED BY RESPONDENTS

| TIME OF DAY* | Percent Respondents Mentioning Time of Day (N=27) |
|---|---|
| Morning (7:00 AM to Noon) | 7 |
| Afternoon (Noon to 5:00 PM) | 15 |
| Early Evening (5:00 PM to 8:00 PM) | 22 |
| Evening (8:00 PM to 11:30 PM) | 37 |
| Late Night (11:30 PM to 7:00 AM) | 19 |
| Anytime | 11 |

*The hours given are approximations derived from the discussions of violence in the interview. Respondents were not asked, nor did they give exact times when violence took place.

### Temporal Dynamics of Violence: Time of Day

In addition to examining the time periods in which violent incidents tend to occur, we can observe characteristic types of violence that take place during different parts of the day.

*Morning and Afternoon.* When violence occurs in the morning or afternoon it usually happens on a day when neither the husband nor wife works, or they work a night shift and are home in the morning. Often times, a morning battle results from the residual conflict from the night before.

Mrs. (55):    He grabbed me and put me against the wall and choked me and the minute he let go I just hit him. He had been drunk the night before and he was

> going out (in the morning). I asked him not to go
> out because there were a few things that needed to
> be done. And he said no. Well, I think I grabbed him
> before he hit me, before he grabbed my throat. I
> think I grabbed him and told him that he was going
> to have to stay home . . . and then he let go of me I
> hit him and he hit me and I hit him back.

Apparently, the groundwork for this battle had been laid
the night before when the husband was drunk. When he
started to go out in the morning, the wife felt that this was
adding insult to injury and either precipitated the attack or
commenced it herself.

Other morning or afternoon violence may occur when the
husband works the "graveyard" shift from 11:00 PM to
7:00 AM. In these instances, conflict may begin when the
wife is aggravated by the husband being under foot, or when
the husband is disturbed by his wife's interference with his
sleep or relaxation time. Mrs. (75) reported that the only
incidents of violence that took place occurred during those
weeks when her husband worked the 11-to-7 shift, or when
he had consecutive days off during the week. She said that
the fights happened during the day, after her husband woke
up. In another family, a fight erupted during the afternoon,
after the husband had awakened and wanted something to
eat.

Mr. (71):     I got up and wanted something to eat and she was
              taking care of the baby. We got into an argument. I
              knocked over the TV tray. . . .

Mrs. (71):    It was a Saturday. He had worked all night and I
              had to take his uniform to the cleaners and run to
              the post office and dragging the baby with me. I was
              tired of taking care of the baby and he wanted his
              dinner. The girl across the street—her husband is
              overseas—she's got 4 kids and it was the first time
              she ever asked me if she could use my washer. I have
              a tendency to let people take advantage of me.

> Instead of telling me why he got mad he picked up
> his lunch and the tray and threw it across the room.
> I started laughing and he got mad. The fight went all
> the way up the stairs and he ended up putting a hole
> in the baby's wall.

In this case, the husband's demand for his dinner conflicted with the wife's daytime chores and led to a free-for-all with throwing of trays, punching holes in walls, and grabbing and pushing each other.

One gets the impression from these interviews that violence in the morning or afternoon typically results from leftover conflict from the previous evening. Violence also can grow out of conflicting time schedules and obligations that arise when both partners are home during the day.

*Evening.* In the section on spatial dynamics of violence, we say that much violence which takes place in the kitchen either commences at dinnertime, or at a time when one of the partners desires to be fed. Mrs. (69) discussed the worst time of the day for her family.

> Mrs. (69):  Evening, it was a very bad time of the day. The man
> comes home from work and the woman has had the
> kids all day. Young children are very fussy at that
> time. Suppertime is not a good time.

One factor contributing to dinnertime violence is the accumulation of frustration from both the wife, who is at home, and the husband, who has been at work. This frustration is supposed to be alleviated by the harmony and tenderness of the family. However, the opposite may occur: the frustration builds to a crescendo during dinnertime when the wife complains to her husband about her day, the husband complains to the wife about his day, and the children (young children) cry, spill their milk, and throw their food. Often times, the children are the recipients of family violence during dinnertime, but other times the combatants may be the husband and wife.

Other evening violence may occur after the children have been put to bed and the husband and wife are alone. At this time, conflict over finances, how to spend leisure time, or drinking may lead to violence.

*Late Night.* Wolfgang's data on homicide reveal that early morning (2:00 AM to 7:59 AM) is the time period where homicide in the home clearly outnumbers homicide out of the home (1958: 365). Thus, when violence happens during these hours, it is usually in the home. We have called this time period late night and have coupled it to the time period from 11:30 PM to 2:00 AM. When family violence occurs in late evening, it usually goes on in the bedroom. The situation surrounding late evening violence is either arguments about sex or alcohol-related incidents of violence (or both). Sometimes late evening violence will commence in the kitchen when an inebriated spouse comes home and demands dinner. The sequence of events described by Mrs. (51) was found in a number of families with late evening, alcohol-related violence.

Mrs. (51):    But when he was drinking, well I couldn't very well greet him with open arms. He'd be gone a day and a half and of course he was bombed when he did come home. He expected to be welcomed home and I was irritated and mad about him spending the money in the first place and he'd hit me . . . how he got up those four flights of stairs I'll never know. He made it to the door, managed to unlock it and he slipped. . . . Well, I used to greet him . . . like how many times he's come home hungry, he hasn't eaten all day, no lunch, no supper. And he'd pop in and take a leftover and start frying himself something. When I was in bed . . . I figured let him be . . . he'll go to bed or he'll fall asleep. Many times it was burnt to a crisp. He fell asleep in a plate of spaghetti, face and all, and yet he was breathing. It got to the point where I got so disgusted, so angry with him . . . I could have just sunk his face in the plate more!

Mrs. (55), sick of her husband coming home drunk and demanding dinner, often tried to provoke her husband to violence to avoid having sex with him.

> Mrs. (55):   I would get upset about his drinking and he would get upset because I didn't feel like getting up and do his cooking and then going back to bed with him.

## Day of the Week

Only 13 of the respondents were able to recall on what day of the week a violent incident took place. The low recall was the result of two factors. First, because the accounts were all retrospective, many people simply could not remember what day a violent episode occurred. Second, some of the high violent families said that violence was an everyday occurrence and that they could not specify one day over another.

Of the 13 respondents who cited a day (or days) when violence transpired, 38% said it usually was on a weekend, 23% said Sunday, and 8% said Saturday. The combined total for all responses indicating violence on a weekend was 69% (Table 9). Even with the limited data on day of the week, the results are similar to the data on assault and homicide.

#### TABLE 9
#### DAY OF THE WEEK OF CONJUGAL VIOLENCE
#### MENTIONED BY RESPONDENTS

| DAY OF THE WEEK | Percent Respondents Mentioning Day of Week  (N=13) |
| --- | --- |
| Sunday | 23 |
| Saturday | 8 |
| Weekend (no day mentioned) | 38 |
| Weekend (combined total) | 69 |
| Weekday | 15 |
| Other:  (pay day, husband's day off, when husband home when working 11-7 shift) | 23 |

Pittman and Handy (1964: 463) state that 55% of assaults happened on the weekend. Pokorny (1965) found that homicides are high on the weekend, with the peak on Saturday. Wolfgang's data on homicide in Philadelphia revealed high rates on Saturdays.

## Temporal Dynamics of Violence: Day of the Week

The analysis of the data on the day of the week indicates the obvious, family violence is high on those days when both spouses are likely to be home. Beyond this, however, the analysis reveals that certain activities take place on the weekend where conflict is likely to flare up. A number of wives reported that alcohol-related violence took place predominantly on the weekend, because this was when their husbands drank the most.

There are other stressful days of the week where families report outbreaks of intrafamily violence. Pay day may be one day where arguments arise over how to divide and spend the family income. Mrs. (55) told that most incidents of violence were on Thursday nights when he got paid. She said she started the fights by asking for money.

Mrs. (55):   It would start over money. It usually started on a Thursday night when he got his pay. And I asked him for some money and then I had to cook him something to eat. He said he didn't have any—he had borrowed money and had to pay it back. Other times he'd give me fifty, and then I'd get mad because I knew I couldn't do anything with it.

Other days when violence may occur are days during the week when the husband has a day off or when the husband is home during the day because of working the 11 PM to 7 AM shift. The dynamics of these incidents have been discussed in the previous section.

## Time of Year

There was almost no recall of what time of year violence typically took place. When respondents did remember incidents they were distributed throughout the year. Some respondents remembered violent fights near or around their birthday or anniversary. One pattern that *did* emerge, however, was that six respondents cited Christmas and New Year's as the time of the year when particularly severe incidents of violence exploded.

Mrs. (13):　　He hit me two days before New Year's. Oh, it was awful. I just felt worse—it was the worst time of the year I ever spent. He brought me here and I was bleeding bad, you know.

Mrs. (59):　　One time, we were going to Manchester and it was around Christmas time, and I was pregnant then. We had a fight. This was going on down Main Street. And he said, "You can get right out here!" I had to call my father to come pick me up.

Mrs. (71):　　(About their neighbor Mr. and Mrs. 70) Well, she was pregnant and it sounds like he's beating her and she's yelling at him . . . New Year's day and they were screaming and yelling and the police finally came.

Mrs. (5):　　I can remember an incident that happened—this was back the first year that I was married to him. It was around Christmas time. He went out and got real drunk and come home and he threw the Christmas tree down, put his fist through the wall and things like that.

It is possible that people recall violence around the holiday season because they are able to associate a particular special date and associated things (Christmas trees going up and so on) with the event, and these events stand out because of these associations and not because any significant feature of those times of the year led to violence. However, it may be that certain times of the year *are* related to incidents of family violence.

There may be a number of factors that contribute to the likelihood of family violence during Christmas and New Year's. First, this is a time of great financial burden on the family. Purchasing Christmas presents takes a giant toll on the family's resources. Second, if the family *cannot* afford to buy the gifts that it desires, the awareness of its financial shortcomings can cause tremendous stress. For the holiday season presents the family with a yearly opportunity to see how it compares to neighbors and friends in terms of financial resources (both how much money they actually have or how much they can borrow). Third, during Christmas and New Year's the idealized images of family harmony, love, and togetherness are fostered by songs, advertisements, and the media. A family with ongoing conflict also may see this in sharp contrast to its own situation. These factors and others may contribute to the holiday season being one of high family conflict and high family violence. Because our data do not provide much support for these assumptions, this hypothesis remains to be investigated in future research.

## PRESENCE OR ABSENCE OF OTHER PEOPLE

There were no cases of violence reported where someone other than a member of the immediate family or a close relative (father or mother) were present during an incident of conjugal violence. In fact, we heard of numerous times where the offender waited until no one was present to instigate an attack.

Mrs. (80):    He's never hit me in front of anyone ... he's too smart for that ... people come over if they know he's around to protect me.

Mrs. (52):    Once, at his father's house he started talking dirty so I started talking dirty and he got mad and when we got out in the car he just hit me across the face.

The usual bystanders during intraspouse violence are the children. In the instances of violence during dinnertime, or during early evening, the children were either present or in the house. Older children were sometimes witnesses and even intervened in outbreaks of conjugal violence later in the evening.

Only one family reported that a member of the nonnuclear family was present during a case of violence, and that was the father of the wife, whom the wife called to intervene for her.

There are a number of reasons why family violence happens when no one else is present. First, violence between family members is considered deviant by the wider society. Thus, the husband does not want to get a reputation as a wifebeater and the wife does not want to be embarrassed by other people seeing her hit or be hit by her husband. One woman told that she never called the police because she was afraid that if they came to her house it would be published in the newspaper.

> Mrs. (61):   I didn't want any of the neighbors to know that he
>              was behaving the way he was. I didn't want anyone
>              around when Ralph was behaving that way . . .
>              that's why I didn't have any neighbors. I didn't even
>              call the police because I was afraid they'd put it in
>              the paper.

Families apparently attempt to maintain an image of harmony, love, and solidarity by postponing violent incidents until there is no one around and trying to hide these incidents from their neighbors.

Another reason why no one outside the family is present during family violence situations is that people who know of violence in a neighbor's family avoid becoming involved. Mrs. (78) speaks about her neighbor Mrs. (80).

> Mrs. (78):   Well, next door, I met a girl and she invited me over
>              one night and asked me to stay with her because her

> husband had come home the previous night and put
> his fist through the glass—he was drunk, very drunk.
> She called me because she thought that her husband
> wouldn't come in if I was there—it didn't work—he
> came in and I immediately took off. If they were
> going to beat each other I wasn't going to be there.

Mrs. (80)'s previous statement described how her husband
did wait for Mrs. (78) to leave before he beat her up.

Mrs. (71) also knows that her neighbor beats his wife. She
too is afraid to get involved because she fears that if the
husband will beat up his wife, he might come next door and
beat up Mrs. (71) if she interferes.

Mrs. (71):    I hear her screaming . . . it sounds like he's throwing
              her against the wall. I don't want to go over or call
              the police on him because he might just come over
              and beat me up. That's why we haven't become
              good friends. I just don't want to be part of that at
              all.

Thus, there is a two-way effort that isolates families that
experience conjugal violence. Violent families isolate themselves for fear of their neighbors finding out, and the neighbors stay away for fear of getting too involved and running
the risk of being hit themselves. In the next chapter, on
violence and family structure, we discuss that this isolation
contributes to both incidents of violence and an escalation of
family violence because it cuts off the family from sources of
social support, social resources, and social control.

Related to isolation from neighbors is the effect that
nonnuclear family members living with a family may have on
the likelihood of physical violence. By the end of the interviews, we had some preliminary notions about the causal
factors involved in family violence such as socialization experience with violence; age, educational, and occupational
prestige differences between husband and wife; family in-

come; religious differences; and other factors that will be discussed in the next chapters. Yet, in three families where conjugal violence clearly was predictable by a combination of these causal factors being present, there were *no* incidents of physical violence between husband and wife. Also, in these three families, there were nonnuclear family members living in on a part-time or full-time basis. One family had a foster child and a father of the husband living with them, while the other two had brothers of the wife living in.

It would seem that the presence of these people served to mitigate against the likelihood of physical violence taking place. It is possible that the husband was afraid to hit his wife with his brother-in-law present, or that these additional people functioned as additional resources (babysitters, rent payers) who reduced what otherwise might have been a stress level that could have led to violence.


## TIME, SPACE, AND FAMILY VIOLENCE: A SUMMARY

The typical situation of family violence is that the location is in the home, usually the kitchen; the time of day is evening or late evening; and it usually occurs on the weekend. These facets of the violent situation contribute to a situation for the family where there is no place to go and no one to turn to (with the exception of the police).

When violence between family members brews and erupts at night, in the home, there often is no escape for either the victim or the offender. If the bars are closed, or one's parents do not live nearby, and the family has few, if any, close friends to turn to, where does one flee to—especially women? In addition, the typical violent family is isolated from its neighbors through the violent family's own actions and through the neighbors' desire not to get involved. Thus, the only resource a victim of family violence can turn to for help is usually the police, who are called in only after blows are struck. The facets of the situation of family violence seem to combine to produce an upward spiral of violence where the only exit may be calling the police, seeking a protective court order, or dissolving the marriage.

## ALCOHOL AND VIOLENCE

An important component of the violent situation is whether or not alcohol is involved. Evidence from previous research on violence and from data in this study (which led to the development of the type "Alcohol-Related Violence" in the previous chapter) suggest that there is a high association between alcohol and violent acts between family members. In the 44 families where violence had occurred, drinking accompanied violence in 21 families (48%). This association between violence and alcohol is slightly higher than that found in studies of homicide and assault. In Wolfgang's research alcohol was present in the victim in only 9% of the criminal homicides; alcohol was present in the offender in 11% of the incidents; and alcohol was present in both offender and victim in 44% of the cases (1958: 136). Wolfgang concluded that homicide by beating had a higher proportion with alcohol present than homicide by any other method (1958: 141). Gillen's study of murder reveals that more than 30% of murderers were drunk at the time of the crime or had been drinking (1946: 87). Guttmacher's (1960) study of murder grouped murders by type. In the type "normal murder," nearly half of the murderers had been drinking before the crime (1960: 8). Finally, Pittman and Handy's study of aggravated assault identified alcohol present in one-fourth of the 41 cases (1964: 467).

The high incidence of alcohol present in family violence indicates that alcohol and family violence are more closely tied than alcohol and other types of violence. Snell, Rosenwald, and Robey (1964), in discussing wifebeating, conclude that wifebeating is quite common among alcoholic men. Our findings support the general conclusion that the offender is often drinking or drunk when he (or she) beats his spouse. Whether the offender is or was an alcoholic is an open question in our interviews, although wives will often label their husbands as alcoholics.

> Mrs. (17):   He's an alcoholic, that is why I know so much about alcoholism. It is rotten, and the sad part of that situation was he got very violent when he was drinking and he would beat me all around the place and the girls used to see it. They'd wake up in the middle of the night. There is no reason for that.

## The Dynamics of Alcohol and Violence

In the previous chapter alcohol-related violence was discussed as a type of family violence. In that section, wives' accounts of violent incidents revealed that in many, if not all, cases of physical violence their husband was drunk.

> Mrs. (66):   The typical incident, nine out of ten times it was usually when there's drinking involved. I don't drink that much and sometimes, he doesn't drink during the week, but sometimes, you know, on weekends. . . .

> Mrs. (18):   It was only when he was drinking.

> Mrs. (79):   And I took the gun away from him. But he went out again and he went out and drank wine and took pills, this sort of stuff he would . . . he got back in the house again, uh, and he drag me outside the door and the people, they didn't know what the heck to do, and then someone called the police and I had him arrested.

> Mrs. (48):   When he had a couple of drinks under his belt— whether it was beer or liquor, especially liquor—he was very, very different. He was rough. Really, it was the cause of his whole problem.

The accounts of wives about husbands who were violent when drunk focus the blame for the violence on alcohol. These wives feel that their husbands are normal when sober, but become mean, violent animals under the influence of liquor. One wife, who had been beaten often and severely, when asked to choose the most serious family problem her family faced, said it was her husband's drinking problem. Thus, most of the wives subscribe to the "conventional wisdom" that alcohol effects people in such a way as to release pent-up violence. The wives feel that if their husbands did not drink, they would not be violent.

There are a number of contextual features of alcohol-related violence. In many of the situations where the husband returns home drunk, he demands food and sex (usually in that order). These circumstances provoke the wife, who is angry that her husband has been drinking and spending budget money on liquor. The wife also is upset because she has to cook for her inebriated spouse. Finally, she often may be repulsed by the thought of having sex with her drunken husband. The wife often refuses to comply with her husband's demands or complies grudgingly. Faced with his wife's refusal to welcome him home with food and sexual favors, the husband often will berate his wife as a poor cook and as frigid. Thus, the fact that the husband has come home drunk sets off primary conflict over his drinking and secondary conflict over financial problems, the role of the wife, and sexual responsiveness. This conflict in many cases leads to violence.

### Alcohol and Violence: Deviance Disavowal

The high association between violence and alcohol traditionally has been explained as a function of alcohol acting as a causal agent in breaking down inhibitions and leading to "out of character" behavior. The literature, which accounts for violence in terms of alcohol acting as a superego solvent (Guttmacher, 1960: 33), and the wives who say that their husband is like Mr. Hyde when he drinks, concur in labeling alcohol as a major causal agent in violent acts.

There are serious problems in positing alcohol as a primary causal agent in interpersonal violence. MacAndrew and Edgerton (1969) have constructed an impressively documented monograph, which cites cases of cultures where drunkenness *is not* followed by disinhibited behavior such as violence. These authors argue that drunken comportment is situationally variable (MacAndrew and Edgerton, 1969: 53) and essentially a learned affair (MacAndrew and Edgerton, 1969: 88). Wolfgang and Ferracuti (1967) also discuss the variable comportment of intoxicated individuals and point out that not all intoxicated subjects become violent. The data from the 80 families also confirm the variability of individual behavior when drinking. In some families, husbands and wives drink without ever becoming violent. In others, violence occurred without any alcohol being drunk. In other families, where violence did occur when the offender was drinking, it also occurred when he or she did not drink.

If alcohol is not a direct causal agent in the occurrence of violence, why then do we find such a high incidence of intrafamily violence where the offender has been drinking? To answer this we need to examine two important functions of alcohol in the violent situation. First, drinking can serve as a means of neutralizing or disavowing (Davis, 1961; McCaghy, 1968) the deviance of hitting a family member. Second, because the conventional wisdom about alcohol is that it causes "out of character" behavior, the drinker can use the period of time when he is drunk as a "time out" (MacAndrew and Edgerton, 1969), where he is not responsible for his actions.

*Disavowal.* It goes without saying that society would label as deviant most instances of conjugal violence. Because of this, and because family violence occurs in the privacy of the home, violence between spouses is often hushed-up (Gribbon, 1972). When the occurrence of violence in the home becomes public knowledge or when it is discussed by family members, the deviancy must be accounted for. A major problem in discussing and accounting for instances of family violence with interviewers, friends, police, lawyers, and judges is sustaining the definition of one self and one's family as normal. In order to disavow the deviance of family violence or other deviant acts such as child molestation, individuals often invoke the explanation that they were drunk and did not know what they were doing (McCaghy, 1968). Thus, alcohol often is associated with accounts of family violence because it allows the aggressor, the victim, and the other family members to orchestrate an account that admits the occurrence of the deviant behavior but maintains the definition of the family as normal by focusing the blame on the alcohol that *caused* the deviant act. The family that accounts for violence by using the theory of alcohol as a disinhibitor can disassociate the offender from the stigma of being a wifebeater. Drinking is widespread in our society and alcoholism is viewed by some as a sickness and, therefore, drinking and alcoholism carry less stigma for the aggressor and the family than does violence. Thus, we find family members claiming that the major family problem is drinking rather than violence. Mrs. (48) is the wife of a teamster:

> Mrs. (48):   I still think his drinking was the most serious problem. Yes, mainly his drinking. I think that if it hadn't have been for his drinking I could have put up with the rest of it. If he hadn't given in and hadn't drunk as much as he did, he would have been all right.

Mrs. (16), wife of an army sergeant, said that his drinking, not his beating her, was the biggest problem in the family.

The offender and the family concur in the assumption that alcohol renders an individual powerless to control his behavior and, thus, whatever happens is not his fault. To correct the problem, it is the drinking that must be attacked. Thus, families that sought help from social work agencies sought help for the drinking problem of the aggressive spouse and not help or counseling concerning aggression and violence.

*Time Out.* The situation of violence defined as "out of character" behavior, where the individual cannot control himself while under the influence of alcohol, becomes real in its consequences when individuals drink in order to provide an excuse for becoming violent. MacAndrew and Edgerton discuss drunken comportment as essentially a learned affair. One of the aspects of drunken comportment that is learned is that drunkenness is a "time out" from the norms and demands of everyday life (1969: 90). An important aspect of the prevailing definition of drinking and drunkenness that has evolved into the conventional wisdom of alcohol as a disinhibitory agent is that the individual who is drunk is not responsible for his actions. There are even legal foundations for this wisdom. While it is quite controversial, there is a legal precedent for reducing the grade or degree of a homicide because the offender was intoxicated (Kiser, 1944: 832).

Wives contribute to the definition of the situation that their husbands are not responsible for what they do when they drink by arguing that their husbands would *never* hit them when sober.

Mrs. (5):      Only when he was drinking would he do that. When he was sober, he was a totally different man.

Husbands too agree that they are different when drunk. Husbands may become remorseful for their violence when sober or deny that anything took place.

Mrs. (17):     He almost choked me to death one night. The next morning he was crying at the table and he said, "I don't know why I did it, because you've never done anything wrong. I don't know why I do it." He was crying and crying. He was really upset. One time he was so drunk, supposedly, he denied it when he sobered up. He said he never did touch me.

It might be argued that the definition of alcohol as an agent that causes out of character behavior is a definition that serves to justify that behavior by relieving the individual from responsibility for his actions. As such, the definition may become causal, in that it could *promote* the behavior by providing, in advance, a standard, socially approved excuse for violent behavior. Thus, individuals who wish to carry out a violent act become intoxicated *in order to carry out the violent act.* Having become drunk and then violent the individual either may deny what occurred ("I don't remember, I was drunk"), or plead for forgiveness ("I didn't know what I was doing"). In both cases he can shift the blame for violence from himself to the effects of alcohol.

There is a rather vicious cycle involved in the association of alcohol and violence. First, society provides the aggressor with a vocabulary of motives (Gerth and Mills, 1953) and techniques for neutralization (Sykes and Matza, 1957) that assures him that he is not responsible for anything he does while drunk. The individual can then become drunk and enjoy a "time out" from the everyday norms that prohibit family violence. Once sober, he can deny the incident or apologize, with the full knowledge that the denial probably will be accepted and that the incident disavowed. He might continue to be in trouble for drinking, but the episode of violence will be relegated to low priority on the family's list of deviant acts.

## Summary

The analysis of the association between alcohol and violence has turned from the traditional focus on the chemical effects of alcohol on the human brain and the resulting behavioral reactions, to a social psychological, sociolinguistic interpretation of the relationship between alcohol and violence. Alcohol leads to violence, in many cases, because it sets off primary conflict over drinking that can extend to arguments over spending money, cooking, and sex. In these cases, drinking may serve as a trigger for long-standing marital disputes and disagreements. Drinking and violence also are related in a complex of verbalizations and justifications for the occurrence of intrafamily violence. The existence of suitable and acceptable justifications for violence serves to normalize and neutralize the violence. These justifications also may play a causal role in family violence by providing, in advance, an excuse for behavior that is normally prohibited by societal and familial norms and standards.

## NOTES

1. The facets of the violent situation that are examined in this chapter were derived from Wolfgang's (1958) analysis of *Patterns of Criminal Homicide*. Dr. Howard Shapiro suggested the examination of whether or not other people were present during violent episodes.

*Chapter 4*

# THE ROSE GARDEN:

# SOCIAL AND FAMILY STRUCTURE

During an extensive discussion of how she hit her husband
and how he hit her back, one woman paused and commented, "Marriage is never all roses, you know." She has
articulated a fact about marriage that is recognized but not
extensively examined by many family sociologists—that the
family is a system characterized by frequent conflict, disrup-
tions, and disorder. Although some students of family life
argue for the investigation of the family using a conflict
model (Sprey, 1969), the dominant theme and content of
family research has been the study of adjustment, harmony,
and stability through the study of mate selection, different
structural compositions of families, cross-cultural compari-
sons of family life, using a consensus-stable equilibrium approach (Sprey, 1969: 700). Traditionally, where marital
conflict is studied, it is usually studied by examining marital
dissolution as an indicator of conflict.

This chapter examines family violence by focusing on the family's location in the social structure and the aspects of family structure that are associated with conjugal violence. By doing this, the chapter makes two contributions to the study of the family. First, this examination is a causal analysis of the facets of the family's location in the social structure and the aspects of family structure that lead to violence. Second, this approach is of fundamental theoretical importance for the sociology of family life because it is one of the few studies to examine *internal* disruption, stress, and crisis, and its impact on the family.[1]

## SOCIAL STRUCTURE AND FAMILY VIOLENCE

The propositions of three theories of interpersonal violence, structural (Coser, 1967), culture of violence (Wolfgang and Ferracuti, 1967), and resource theory (Goode, 1971), agree in predicting that conjugal violence is more likely in families occupying positions in the lower levels of the social structure. The structural theory of violence asserts that one should find more violence among families who are in lower social positions because they suffer more frustrations and blocked goals than do families on the higher rungs of the social ladder. Cultural theory of violence proposes that among certain groups or subcultures there are norms and cultural values that approve of violence rather than define it as deviant. The cultural theory of violence locates these proviolent norms among individuals and groups in the lower social strata; and thus, this group comprises a subculture of violence. Resource theory argues that the greater resources a person can command, the more force he can muster, but the less he will actually deploy force in an overt manner (Goode, 1971: 628). The theory states that violence is used as a resource when other resources are lacking; thus, a family member that has little prestige, money, and power suffers greater frustration and bitterness and resorts to violence more (Goode, 1971: 633).

Although these three theories use different propositions, they argue for essentially the same result—people with less education, occupational status, and income will be more violent than people with more education, occupational status, and income. Little empirical data accompany the theories on violence between family members, however. The first part of this section on social structure and family violence examines the family's location in the social structure by analyzing the spouses' education, occupational status, and total family income and tests the assumption that families located in the lower portions of the social strata have more conjugal violence. The final part of the section focuses on a facet of violent families that was discussed briefly in the previous chapter—isolation from neighbors and *social* resources.

## The Violent Family's Location in the Social Structure

We are concerned in this section with examining how violent families differ from nonviolent families in terms of age, education, occupational status, income, and religion. In other words, are violent families characterized by a particular location in the social structure[2] that make them violence-prone?

*Age.* There is conjugal violence among family members of all ages. Violence between family members is not just an act of youth. An important finding is that the age group where there is the most conjugal violence is from 41 to 50 years old (Table 10). Thus, for both husband and wife, violence is not a phenomenon found only among young brides and grooms who are trying to cope with getting used to being married, early career contingencies, and transition from late adolescence to adulthood. The most violent age group includes those husbands and wives who are approaching both middle age and the middle of their occupational careers.

The findings that conjugal violence is most common among the middle age group corresponds to Snell, Rosenwald, and Robey's (1964) data on wifebeating, where the average age of the beaten wife was 37 years.

## TABLE 10
## PERCENT OF CONJUGAL VIOLENCE BY SEX AND AGE

|  | Husband's Age | | | | Wife's Age | | | |
|---|---|---|---|---|---|---|---|---|
|  | 19-30 (N=30) | 31-40* (N=17) | 41-50* (N=19) | 51+ (N=11) | 19-30 (N=34) | 31-40 (N=22) | 41-50 (N=17) | 51+ (N=7) |
| No Violence | 40 | 65 | 37 | 54 | 47 | 45 | 35 | 57 |
| Infrequent** Violence | 43 | 12 | 21 | 27 | 38 | 18 | 24 | 29 |
| Frequent*** Violence | 17 | 24 | 42 | 18 | 15 | 36 | 41 | 14 |

*excludes husbands deceased at time of interview
**from once in a marriage to six times a year
***from monthly to daily

*Education.* Analyzing the relationship between education and conjugal violence, we find an inverse relation between husband's education and conjugal violence. The most conjugal violence occurs where the husband's education is lowest while the more educated husbands are involved in less violence with their wives (Table 11). The same relation does not

## TABLE 11
## PERCENT OF CONJUGAL VIOLENCE BY EDUCATION

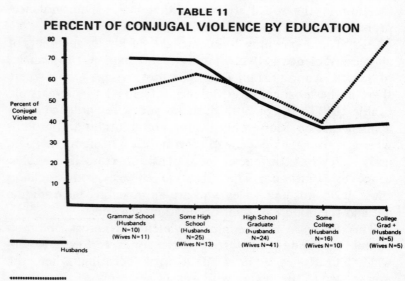

hold for wife's education. The most violence occurs in families where the wife has had at least some high school education. There is also a rather high level of violence among those women who are college graduates. This leads to a hypothesis that these women have more education than their husbands. This will be taken up when family violence and family structure are examined.

Conjugal violence is most frequent where the husband has had at least some high school education (Table 12). It might be surmised that, at least for husbands, the stresses of being a high school drop-out are more constant than the pressures and frustrations on husbands with only a grammar school education.

The association between low education and high family violence also has been found by Komarovsky (1967). Komarovsky's data reveal that violent quarrels were mentioned as a mode of conflict by 27% of the husbands with under 12 years of school and by 17% of husbands with 12 years. For wives, 33% with under 12 years education mentioned violence while only 4% with 12 years education discussed violent quarrels (1967: 366).

**TABLE 12**

**PERCENT OF FREQUENT CONJUGAL VIOLENCE BY EDUCATION**

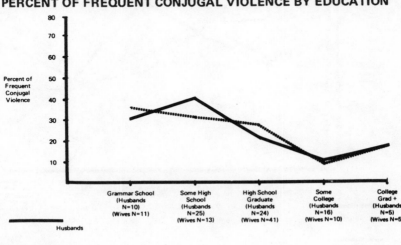

*Occupational Status.* The data on occupational status[3] and conjugal violence show that violence is prevalent when the husband's occupational status is low (Table 13). However, those husbands with medium occupational status—carpenters, milkmen, machine operators, and so on, are most likely to be involved in incidents of family violence with their wives. Husbands with low occupational status—truck drivers, laborers, and so on, were involved in more frequent violence (Table 14). It was expected that unemployed husbands would be the most violent based on the assumption that unemployment leads to role stress in the family, which leads to violence. Although there is violence in the families where the husband is not employed, it is less than where the husband has a job with low or medium occupational status. The stress of being employed in a low or medium status job would appear to be more than that of being unemployed. We might posit that men working on low or medium status jobs may be involved in stressful competition both to keep the job and to advance, and this can lead to longer work hours, more strain, and the result could be conflict and violence at home.

**TABLE 13**
**PERCENT OF CONJUGAL VIOLENCE BY OCCUPATIONAL STATUS**

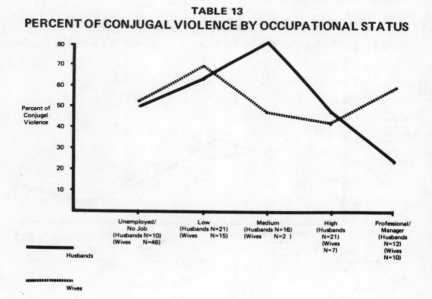

**TABLE 14**
## PERCENT OF FREQUENT CONJUGAL VIOLENCE
## BY OCCUPATIONAL STATUS

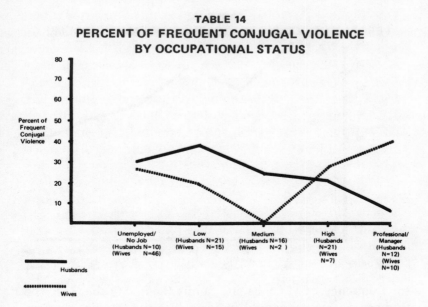

Wives with low status jobs and wives with professional-managerial status occupations are the most violence-prone (Table 13). On the one hand, working at a menial job may lead to violence because this job may hold little intrinsic reward and the wife only may be working to make ends meet in her family. In addition, the dual roles of worker-homemaker may create stress within the family when the wife who works all day has to come home and make dinner, make the beds, clean the house, do the laundry, and put the children to sleep. On the other hand, the high levels of violence in families where a wife holds a professional position may be a function of conflict over her status being higher than her husband's and the duality of roles. This will be discussed in the section on family structure.

*Income.* There is an inverse relation between income and conjugal violence, where violence is higher with low income and lower with high income. The highest incidence of violence is found at the extreme low end of total family income (Table 15). Violence is the most frequent in the $3,000 to $4,999 group, but the same general inverse relationship holds

TABLE 15
PERCENT OF CONJUGAL VIOLENCE BY FAMILY INCOME

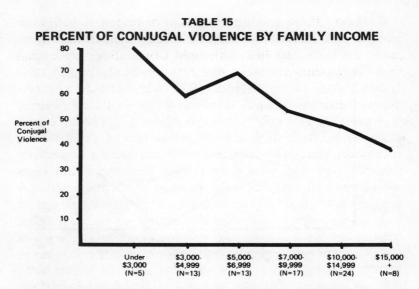

for frequency of violence and family income (Table 16). The findings on income would indicate that the families that are under the greatest stress are those who are absolutely deprived financially. For them luxuries are out of the question and their daily struggle is to pay for food and the rent.

TABLE 16
PERCENT OF FREQUENT CONJUGAL VIOLENCE
BY FAMILY INCOME

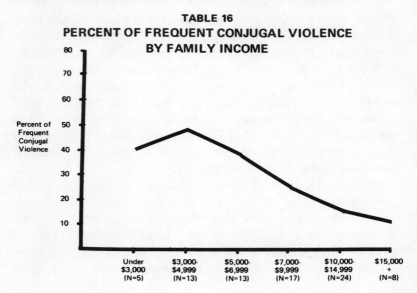

*Religion.* There was no indication or reason to believe in advance that Catholics would be more violent than Protestants in their families, although Goode does state that Catholic parents are more likely to physically punish their children than are Protestants (1971: 629). The data on religious affiliation of family members reveal no great difference between Catholics and Protestants (Table 17). The difference in terms of frequency may be a function of the sampling technique, where police cases were drawn from a less heavily Catholic city than were agency cases (and the police cases were more violent). The major findings in this examination is the generally high level of violence in families where one or both of the spouses is an agnostic, atheist, or has no religion. There may be a number of explanations for this level of violence, some of which may tend to make this finding an emotionally charged issue. Some ideas come from examining data on religious affiliation and divorce which reveal that the highest divorce rate is for families where neither spouse had a religious affiliation (Monahan and Kephart, 1954). Among the reasons (1) these individuals are less conventional people and therefore, they are less bound to society's "don't hit" and "stay married" conventions. (2) If these individuals are less conventional, they also are less bound to conventions and

TABLE 17
**PERCENT OF CONJUGAL VIOLENCE BY SEX AND RELIGION**

|  | Husband's Religion* | | | Wife's Religion* | | |
|---|---|---|---|---|---|---|
|  | Catholic (N=37) | Protestant (N=35) | None (N=7) | Catholic (N=42) | Protestant (N=32) | None (N=5) |
| No Violence | 49 | 48 | 14 | 43 | 56 | 0 |
| Infrequent** Violence | 32 | 23 | 29 | 36 | 9 | 80 |
| Frequent*** Violence | 19 | 29 | 57 | 21 | 34 | 20 |

*excludes the one Jewish family classified as "infrequent violence"
**from once in a marriage to six times a year
***from monthly to daily

norms regarding marital roles (expectations, obligations, fidelity, and so on) and there may be greater conflict and greater divorce. (3) The no-religion families and individuals might be a rootless sector of the population who are lacking in social supports and social constraints. (4) This no-religion group may be predominantly drawn from the lower extremes of the socioeconomic ladder, and thus, more subject to the stresses that can lead to divorce and violence.

*Structural Stress.* Throughout this section on the location of the violent family in the social structure, it has been asserted that certain locations produce more stress than do others. The informal interviews produced a number of discussions about the stresses and frustrations produced by low education, unemployment or low status jobs, and lack of financial resources.

One consequence of low education is unemployment or sporadic employment. Although it was found that violence was lower in families with unemployed husbands than in families where husbands had low or middle status jobs, unemployment still produces stress for the husband and the family. Roger Tredgold, a British psychologist, found that unemployed men often beat their wives. Tredgold stated that frustrations and tensions arise in homes when men are unemployed (*Parade,* 1971: 13).

Husbands are not the only family members who suffer from the frustrations of being unemployed. Mrs. (16), a 41-year-old housewife who has been beaten quite often by her husband, discussed the stress that they were under when her husband was looking for a job.

> Mrs. (16): He's worried about what kind of job he's gonna get and how's he gonna support the family. I think I worry about it more than he does. . . . He gets very frustrated. He gets quite angry sometimes. I think he gets angry at himself for not providing what he feels that we need and he has to take it out on somebody and it, like I seem to be the source.

Seasonal or sporadic employment also causes financial problems and stress for families. Mr. (8) is a laborer who is in and out of work and who has hit his wife on a number of occasions.

Mrs. (8):     Well, we had financial problems. My husband was in and out of work at different times. I would say he had bad luck. He's a good worker, but several places where he worked went out of business. He worked for a couple of places that folded up right after the other. And then he went to work for a local place and that went out of business too. Unbelievable. So we've had problems that way.

A product of unemployment, or working for low wages, are the inevitable arguments about money.

Mrs. (75):    There's never enough money. He either spends too much or I spend too much or we're short of money and the tension builds up because you can't meet the bills. You snap at each other just because of the tension.

One result of having low education and low financial resources is the inability of the family to withstand much stress. In two separate families conjugal violence followed on the heels of the husband losing his driver's license or truck, both of which were the key to his job.

Mrs. (16):    One time he lost his license and he took the car and went away. When he came back he slapped me around. I got upset about that. He came back and was very abusive and he hit me with his hands.

Mrs. (48):    When things got down and he couldn't take them or the bill collectors ... he got depressed. ... One afternoon, I think it was summertime, if I remember right. Because I remember they had taken the truck away from him because he couldn't keep up the payments. He lost his temper and smashed everything he could find.

In summary, certain positions in the social structure lead to more stress and frustration and the families in these positions lack educational and financial resources to cope with stress. This can lead to conflict and ultimately violence.

## Summary

The examination of social structure and family violence confirms the propositions made by structural, cultural, and resource theories—violence is the most common in families who have low education, low income, and low occupational status. Generally, the relationship between the measures of social position and family violence are inverse relations. The exceptions are the relationship between occupational status and violence and the measures of the wife's social position (education, occupational status) and conjugal violence.

The data on the husband's occupational status and conjugal violence produce an inverted U-shaped curve, rather than the plot found for education and income. Violence is not the most common among those husbands who are unemployed, rather it is the highest among families where the husband has a medium status job. This indicates that violence may be likely to occur in relatively disadvantaged families.

Examining the association between the wife's education and conjugal violence and the wife's occupational status and conjugal violence reveals that in both incidence and frequency of violence the wife is less violent than the husband with lower education and occupational status and *more* violent than the husband when she has high education and occupational status. We hypothesize that these curvilinear relationships are produced by family organizational effects rather than a socioeconomic effect per se. This will be taken up in the section of family structure and family violence.

## Violent Families and Their Nonviolent Neighbors:
## A Comparison

This section examines whether or not the violent families are in fact "disadvantaged" by comparing violent families to nonviolent neighbors. There were 22 families where conjugal violence occurred and there was no violence between the neighboring spouses. Neighbors often comprise a reference group or part of the "generalized other" by which a family can measure their own status and economic well-being. When one speaks of keeping up with the Joneses, the "Joneses" are often the next-door neighbors. In this comparison, the neighbors are either a selected match for a family chosen from agency or police files (17 families), or a nonviolent police or agency family living near a family randomly chosen and violent (5 families).

The major difference between violent families is in the occupational status of the husbands (Table 18). Violent family husbands have lower occupational status than their

### TABLE 18
### COMPARISON OF FAMILIES WITH CONJUGAL VIOLENCE TO NEIGHBORS WITH NO CONJUGAL VIOLENCE
### (By Percent)

|  | (N=22 Pairs) |
|---|---|
| Violent Family Husband has less education than neighbor | 64 |
| Violent Family Wife has less education than neighbor | 41 |
| Violent Family Husband has lower occupational status than neighbor | 82 |
| Violent Family has lower total income than neighbor | 50 |

neighbors in 84% of the cases. It would seem, at least for occupational status, violent husbands are not keeping up with the Joneses. This may lead to two sources of stress and frustration. First, a violent husband who looks at his position vis-à-vis his neighbor will find that he has less prestige and status. In addition, his shortcomings may be pointed out by his own wife. A wife may use her husband's inferior job to attack his self-esteem in the course of a family conflict. In terms of family income, violent families seem to do no worse than their neighbors—they make less income than their neighbors in 50% of the cases and as much, if not more, in the other half of the cases.

An interesting finding is that violent family husbands have less education than their nonviolent neighbors 64% of the time while 59% of the violent family wives have as much or more education than nonviolent wives. We find here that when the husband possesses deficient educational resources it affects intrafamily violence much more than when the wife has deficient educational resources. In fact, the wife's comparatively high educational achievement (compared to her neighbors) may tend to promote rather than to mitigate against violence.

When comparing violent families to nonviolent neighbors, the chief finding is that the deprivation of the violent families is a social deprivation of the husband. In violent families, husbands are less educated and have less occupational prestige than their nonviolent neighbors. They may be able to afford the same house or apartment as their neighbors, they may drive the same model car, but their occupational and educational calling cards are inferior to their neighbor's.

## Social Isolation and Conjugal Violence

During the interviewing when respondents were asked to discuss their neighbor's family problems, and again when respondents were asked who they turned to for help in coping with their own family problems, it became evident that a large number of the respondents did not know their neighbors well, had few friends in the community, and rarely visited with neighbors or friends. Other respondents had many friends among their neighbors, visited their neighbors often, turned to their neighbors for help, and were able to discuss numerous family problems in the neighborhood with the detail and elaboration of a soap opera.

The interviews with members of the 80 families gave the impression that the violent families were almost completely cut off from their neighbors. They did not know them, they had few friends in the neighborhood, they almost never visited their neighbors, and in short, had few social resources in the community who they could turn to for help when they encountered family problems. While violent families did not know their neighbors, their nonviolent neighbors were knowledgeable about their neighbors and had many friends in the neighborhood. An example of the difference in the comparison between two neighbors—Mrs. (44) and Mrs. (45). Mrs. (44) owns her own home and has never hit or been hit by her husband. Mrs. (45) lives across the street and has been involved in some serious knockdown, drag-out physical brawls with her husband. Mrs. (44) discusses her neighbors:

Mrs. (44):    I like the neighborhood quite well, surprisingly well for just having moved here two years ago. They have been quite friendly and hospitable. The woman next door is my close friend. She is quite a bit older and has children who are married and are my age. But she has been a very good friend. It's a friendly neighborhood.

In contrast, Mrs. (45) knows few neighbors, has few friends, and does not do much socializing with her neighbors.

Mrs. (45):    I don't bother with them and they don't bother with me. I don't mean it that way . . . we say hello or they might wave. I'm not the type that goes from

> one house to the next. I'm not that type of social
> gatherer anyway. We help them, they help us, things
> that are needed. They are good neighbors.

Mrs. (45) thinks that they are good neighbors, but doesn't
know the first thing about them. Mrs. (44), however, was
able to inventory the family problems in many of her neighbors' families.

There are two possible causal sequences that account for
violent families' social isolation. In Chapter 3, it was reported that Mrs. (61) stated that she isolated herself from her
neighbors because she was embarrassed by her husband's
drinking and violence. Thus, one sequence would be that
marital conflict leads to violence, which leads to isolation.
The second possible sequence is that social isolation precedes
family violence and is a causal agent in making a family
violence-prone. In these instances, certain families are isolated from their neighbors and, thus, have few social contacts
or social "resources" in the community. When a stressor
event occurs that leads to a family problem or family conflict, these isolated families have few people they can turn to
for advice or for help. They lack what could be called a
"social safety valve." For instance, in one family a wife may
be sick and need help with taking care of her children. If she
has friends in the neighborhood or community, she may call
them and ask for assistance. In another family, a wife may be
sick and need help with the children and not have anyone to
call to help her out. Her problems are then multiplied and
this could lead to conflict between her and the children or
strife between her and her husband.

There are indications in the interview data that the second
causal sequence is the one which applies in most cases of
isolation and violence. Violent families are characterized by
social isolation and do not account for this as a result of
breaking off interaction to avoid embarrassment. They explain their lack of friends with a variety of reasons that are
not related to violence. Mrs. (20) works as a hostess and has
been involved in some incidents of violence.

Mrs. (20):    No, I know maybe two families down at the other
              end, but the only people that I know close by is
              across the hall in this building . . . but I don't know
              too many people.

Mrs. (6) is a hairdresser who was beaten severely by her
husband a few times.

Mrs. (6):     I think I've always been busy, you know, even my
              next-door neighbor right here; I think I've been in
              her house once in ten years. And she's always after
              me to go over and have coffee with her but I don't
              have the time.

Mrs. (51) discussed being involved in over 50 incidents of
physical violence in the past year. She works as a waitress.

Mrs. (51):    I don't bother with the neighbors because I work
              and being the mother of five I haven't the time to. I
              mean I talk and say hello to familiar faces but that's
              about it. I don't visit and no one comes here.

Social isolation is found not only when the wife works. In
many instances where the wife did not work and was home
all day, she still had few social contacts in the community.

It is an empirical question *why* these families become
isolated in the first place, but it does seem that social aliena-
tion could be an important factor involved in conjugal violence. Social isolation of a family can mean no one to turn to
for help or advice in times of crisis and, thus, the crisis may
escalate into a conflict and violence. Isolation also may
deprive the spouses of a "neutral zone" to escape to in case
of escalating conflict. As we found in the examination of the
violent situation, violence occurs in the home, in rooms and
during times when there is no place to escape to. If one of
the potential combatants has a friend next door she (or he)
can either call for the neighbor to intervene or run to the
neighbor's house in order to get out of harm's way.

## FAMILY STRUCTURE AND FAMILY VIOLENCE

The vision of the family living in a rose garden may be beautiful and compelling, but when one enters or falls into the real and metaphoric rose garden, one finds quite another thing. It is incredible to find couples waiting until after they promise to love, honor, and cherish each other to begin assaulting each other. In only one family did we find violence that had occurred before the couple exchanged their nuptial vows. In two families the wives dated, married, divorced, dated again, and remarried the same man and violence occurred *only* during the times when they were legally married. The fact that conjugal violence typically occurs between the combatants only when they are legally married[4] indicates two aspects of familial violence. One is that it is possible that violence between marital partners is considered normative to the extent that it is not permissable to hit the same person outside the bounds of matrimony. Second, violence between individuals involved in intimate love relations is likely only when these two individuals are involved in the structural situation of family life with its concomitant stresses and frustrations and surrounded by the inherent complex role relations and role expectations.

It was not the purpose of this research to examine attitudes towards conjugal violence; therefore, we cannot support with data the notion that violence between spouses, in part, may be a function of cultural norms that give tacit approval to a certain level of conjugal violence but which label as deviant any violence outside matrimony. This research deals with the *behavior* in question by examining the structural characteristics of the family that are associated with intrafamily violence.

### Family Roles and Family Violence

Goode's (1971) theoretical work on family violence and O'Brien's (1971) empirical data and analysis support the hypothesis that violence is more prevalent in families where the husband fails to possess the achieved skills and status upon which his ascribed superior status as head of the household is based. Goode argues that an individual will deploy force when he has few resources at his command (1971: 628). O'Brien (1971: 694) states that violence is most common when the husband-provider is deficient relative to the wife-mother in achieved status characteristics (such as education and occupational status).

The findings on the difference between husband and wife in educational attainment and occupational status support the hypothesis that violence is more prevalent in families where the husband's education and occupational status are lower than his wife's (Table 19 and Table 20). It is interesting to note that the husband's inferior status vis-à-vis his wife is associated with violence only in terms of achieved status characteristics. Looking at the data on the difference between husband and wife for an ascribed characteristic—age— shows that there is less violence when the wife is older than when the husband is older (Table 21).

There are two possible explanations that account for the husband's status inconsistency (high-ascribed status of worker-provider, low-achieved status in education and occupation) being associated with acts of conjugal violence. One explanation that has been proposed by both Goode and O'Brien is that violence is deployed in the family as it is in society—by a superior status group (husbands) on an inferior group (wives and children) when the legitimacy of the superior group's status is questioned (O'Brien, 1971: 695). An alternative explanation is that when the husband cannot adequately fulfill his expected role as worker-provider this is a source of frustration. Aggression may follow on the heels of continued frustration in meeting societal expectations (O'Brien, 1971: 696). Our data cannot adequately support one proposition rather than the other: the interviews reveal that elements of both positions are present in families where the husband fails to meet the role requirements of worker-provider/husband-father.

## TABLE 19
## CONJUGAL VIOLENCE BY EDUCATIONAL DIFFERENCE BETWEEN SPOUSES

|  | Educational Difference | | |
| --- | --- | --- | --- |
|  | Husband More Education (N=35) | Same (N=22) | Wife More Education (N=23) |
| No Violence | 57% | 41% | 30% |
| Infrequent* Violence | 20 ⎫ | 27 ⎫ | 43 ⎫ |
| Frequent** Violence | 23 ⎭ 43 | 32 ⎭ 59 | 26 ⎭ 69 |

*from once in a marriage to six times a year
**from monthly to daily

## TABLE 20
## CONJUGAL VIOLENCE BY DIFFERENCE IN OCCUPATIONAL STATUS BETWEEN SPOUSES

|  | Difference in Occupational Status | | |
| --- | --- | --- | --- |
|  | Husband Higher Status (N=54) | Same (N=5) | Wife Higher Status (N=21) |
| No Violence | 48% | 40% | 38% |
| Infrequent* Violence | 28 ⎫ | 40 ⎫ | 24 ⎫ |
| Frequent** Violence | 24 ⎭ 52 | 20 ⎭ 60 | 38 ⎭ 62 |

*from once in a marriage to six times a year
**from monthly to daily

## TABLE 21
## CONJUGAL VIOLENCE BY DIFFERENCE IN AGE BETWEEN SPOUSES

|  | Age Difference | | |
| --- | --- | --- | --- |
|  | Husband Older (N=48) | Same (N=19) | Wife Older (N=13) |
| No Violence | 42% | 47% | 54% |
| Infrequent* Violence | 31 ⎫ | 32 ⎫ | 15 ⎫ |
| Frequent** Violence | 27 ⎭ 58 | 21 ⎭ 53 | 31 ⎭ 46 |

*from once in a marriage to six times a year
**from monthly to daily

In families where the husband's education and occupational status were inferior to his wife's, there was evidence that this contributed to the husband becoming quite sensitive to the legitimacy of his status as the head of the family. In a number of instances, a violent attack took place after the husband's superordinate position in the family was either challenged or undermined. In one instance, the decision as to who got the first piece of a birthday cake set off an explosion. Mr. (17) is unemployed and is less educated than his wife.

> Mrs. (17):   We were having a birthday party and my father was there. My father was working that day and had to be at work by three o'clock. It was around two-thirty and we were cutting the cake. Well, I had my son blow out the candles and make a wish and then help make the first cut. I had him give the first piece to my father because he had to go to work. My husband stormed out of the house . . . he came back loaded that night simply because my father had the first piece of birthday cake instead of him. . . . That was the first time he broke my wrist.

Incredibly, the same thing happened to another family.

> Mrs. (61):   One time, one of the girls had a birthday and I invited these folks out for a party. I was raised that when you had guests you would serve them first. My husband raised the roof and put the people out because he wasn't served first.

Thus, even symbolic challenges to one's superior position are likely to set off violent confrontations. But, there are more concrete instances of clashes when the father fails to possess the status and skills expected of his position. When direct challenges are made in these instances they often result in violence. Sometimes a wife challenges her husband's decision because she wants more personal freedom and more authority in her family. Mrs. (52) was better educated than her husband and wanted to have some say in what she did with her time. This often led to conflict and hitting between her and her husband.

> Mrs. (52):   He wanted to be boss. Like if I wanted to go out someplace—he was working nights at the time—and I wanted to go to the beach with some girls . . . well, he didn't think it was right. So he says, "Well, you're not taking the car." And I said, "I am," and so I did. And he was mad just because I went and we weren't doing anything wrong . . . I wanted things my own way and he thought he was going to be head because he was the man.

Mr. (52) was like many husbands who tried to control their wives' activities by restricting or trying to restrict their wives' access to the car and to money. When the wife disobeyed it usually meant trouble and violence.

When a wife seeks to dissolve a marriage because she no longer can stand to be married to her husband, she sometimes can be blocked by a husband who controls the financial and social resources of the family. We interviewed some wives who were contemplating divorce but could not consummate it because they felt they might be punished by their husbands, who could throw them out of the house, cut off their funds, take away their children, and so on. In other families where the wife was better educated than her husband, had a better paying job, and was the de facto head of the household, the divorce was easier to obtain. But, in these cases, the reaction of the husband was a violent one. One husband responded to his wife's serving papers on him by breaking into her apartment and almost choking her to death. Another wife was continually assaulted by her husband during the separation, litigation, and aftermath of the divorce. In these cases, the husband appears to be deploying violence as a last means of controlling the behavior of his wife. An incredible case of this occurred in Florida as reported by the *Boston Globe* (December 23, 1972: 2):

Jacksonville, Fla.—A couple drew pistols and began a blazing gun battle during a divorce court hearing yesterday. It left the woman dead and the wounded husband charged with murder, police said. "Witnesses said he didn't want the divorce but she said she was going to leave it to the judge," Gould said. "He then pulled out a pistol and fired."

Family violence occurs not only when the husband role is challenged but also when the father role is taken to task—particularly when it is the child who does the challenging. Numerous incidents of father-to-child violence occur when the children turn against their father. When the children are in their teens, the violence may be two-way—as in the family of Mrs. (51).

Mrs. (51):     The children turned against him. That was enough for him to turn against them. They'd yell, "Leave her alone, don't touch Mommy" and "Mommy, he hit you!" Then he'd start hitting them—then his authority as a father used to take over. All of a sudden he was your father, "You don't talk to me like that. . . ." The oldest son has hit the father to leave me alone. . . . My oldest one really shamed into him, he said, "You're going to come home, sure, you'll give your pay to Mommy. You want her to manage the money and pay all the bills. Your pay won't even be enough to cover the bills." And I think it really shamed him to have his only son say that—at the time Arnie was only 13.

Violence frequently erupts when the wife berates her husband because he is a poor provider. His shortcomings produce conflict, which in turn leads to violence. Mrs. (68) discusses the severe arguments that precipitate her husband hitting her.

Mrs. (68):     We had a really bad argument a couple of weeks ago. I was out of work and I had come home one day—I had expected to be laid off—and he was sitting in the chair. And I thought, this wouldn't

happen if you (her husband) had gone out years ago
and gotten a really good job. I threw this up in his
face. It doesn't do any good. . . . For one thing, my
husband is an alcoholic. I have had it brought up
several times by him, "You knew I drank when you
married me." To this day I do not have a good
answer. I was only 20 then, I'm 54 now. I thought I
could change him. Then again, he does not have an
education. That is a drawback to the fact that he
does not have a steady job. I think it stinks to have
to go from one job to another. We argue about it
constantly. I think it is very depressing. I've lived in
this city all my life. I see these people that I have
gone to school with and they have progressed, and
they have jobs and homes, and I have nothing—and
that really does upset me.

Apparently, in addition to the two explanations provided
by Goode and O'Brien, the husband's inferior educational
and occupational status lead to violence by causing extensive
family conflict over the husband's inability to meet his wife's
expectations concerning her desired life style. Wives often
complain that their husband's lack of ambition is a constant
source of conflict.

Mrs. (77):    My husband is the type who has no ambition. He
has a little. But he doesn't realize that he's making
70 or 80 dollars a week. We can't live on that. We
have a new car. I think he should look for something better. I was working for a time. I didn't like
the type of work I was doing for the simple fact
that I don't like being a salesgirl. It irked me but it
was the only thing that I could get. So I asked him
if he would just try and get another job.

There is evidence in the accounts of violent incidents that
violence in families where the husband has less education and
occupational status than his wife is often a function of the
husband's frustration with his inability to provide adequately

for his family. Mrs. (16) was quoted earlier as saying that her husband would get quite frustrated with his difficulties in providing for his family and would take it out on her. Mrs. (76) also mentioned that her husband was quite frustrated and jealous because his wife was making more money and had a better job.

In summary, the husband's inferior achieved status is a source of frustration for both himself and his wife. His lack of education may hold him back from occupational mobility and block both his and his wife's aspirations. When the husband's status is inferior to his wife's, he becomes vulnerable to verbal critiques about his low level of achievement. Thus, his status may be the causal agent in the conflict that leads to violence. In addition, his status makes him sensitive to actual or perceived threats to the dominant position that society prescribes for the man of the house. His reaction to perceived or actual challenges may initiate or escalate intra-familial conflict. In short, it may not be fruitful to think of the relationship between the husband's status inconsistency and family violence as a case of either one causal proposition or another, but rather the dynamics of violence suggest that violence is a product of a combination of frustrations, lack of resources, and the accompanying conflict that arises when husbands fail to possess the necessary status and skills expected of the husband-provider role.

## Role Reversal

An outgrowth of the husband's inferior achieved status in comparison to his wife's may be a complete reversal of roles in the family whereby the wife becomes the head of the household and the locus of power and the husband retreats into a passive-submissive role. This aspect of family structure has been cited as a pattern associated with conjugal violence by some researchers who have examined wifebeating. Snell, Rosenwald, and Robey (1964) assert that wifebeaters are typically passive, indecisive, and sexually inadequate while their wives are aggressive, masculine, and masochistic. Schultz

(1960) also found that the wifebeater is submissive and passive while his wife is domineering, outspoken, and masculine. Palmer's (1955) narrative of a wifebeater described him as a submissive individual who is dominated by his wife and who finally strikes her.

A number of violent families displayed these characteristics of role reversal where the wife had taken the reins of the family. These wives typically described their husbands as immature and abrogating all responsibility for anything in the family.

> Mrs. (6):    Well, like you asked me before who was the head of the household. Well, in my case he's never had any responsibility. Let's put it this way. I've had to shoulder everything. And my husband is very immature so I've more or less had to shoulder everything. . . . He doesn't think like a man his age—he thinks more like a child.

> Mrs. (13):    And I handle all the money so that makes it—well, if he doesn't have the money to buy what he wants, it's my fault. . . . You know, it's enough to make you throw up!

One thing that happens in this role reversal is that the husband who has had trouble adequately filling the husband-provider role takes out his frustrations on his wife. In the families where the role reversal was complete, violence often followed confrontations where the husband claimed that the wife was to blame for a lack of money or when something else went wrong. Mrs. (10) describes a serious beating that followed one of these confrontations.

> Mrs. (10):    In our marriage he feels that I am totally responsible for anything that has ever happened. He feels that he is not responsible for anything. . . . The child born with medical troubles was my fault by him. Oh

> yea, I could have prevented that. Anything is my
> fault. If I get emotionally upset. He—the time he hit
> me was one time of that.

This aspect of role reversal, which has received attention in
the psychiatric analysis of family violence, appears to be a
special case of family structure where the husband is deficient in educational attainment and occupational status.

### Violence and Pregnancy

A startling discovery in the study of conjugal violence was
that a large number of women stated that they were beaten
while pregnant. In 10 of the 44 families where violence
occurred, wives reported being beaten when pregnant. This is
startling because one does not ordinarily think of an association between creating a life and physical violence. And yet, as
the data show, there is a relationship here between being
pregnant and being hit. In fact, this relationship shows up in
other locales. Steinmetz and Straus (1974) were unable to
find mention of any conjugal violence in American fiction
(except where the combatants were foreign, in some other
way deviant such as criminals, or where they were not legally
married). Yet, I was able to locate two works of fiction
where there is conjugal violence—*The Godfather* and *Gone
With the Wind*. What is particularly interesting about this is
that in both instances a husband beats his *pregnant* wife.

It is quite difficult to begin to explain why wives are
beaten when they are pregnant. There is some indication that
sexual tensions and frustrations are involved in violent
attacks on a pregnant spouse. Mrs. (10) tells of what she felt
were some rather curious sexual habits of her husband and
how he frequently beat her when she was pregnant.

> Mrs. (10):   He hit me when I was pregnant—that was his past-
> time. Plus, he . . . his sex life too. He's, um—I found
> out afterwards—I don't know what you call it a

> homosexual or what. We would have sex relations
> and he would have a jar of vaseline. If things weren't
> going just right he would stop and he would go into
> the bathroom and masturbate. I really don't know
> how I got pregnant. I think it was Immaculate
> Conception!

Other husbands, particularly husbands who felt forced to
marry a pregnant woman, may feel increasing stress as the
baby approaches (or as the wife swells). Mrs. (70) tells of
how her husband was under tremendous strain because he
had had to get married and was about to become a father.

> Mrs. (70):    Our problem was getting married and having a baby
> so fast ... that produced a great strain. ... I wasn't
> ready and he wasn't ready. I had the baby 6 months
> after we were married.

The literature on parenthood as family crisis (LeMasters,
1957; Dyer, 1963; Hobbs, 1965) reveals that becoming a
parent for the first time does lead to family crisis. In our
study we find that in some families, having a child leads to
crisis and violence *even before* the child is born.

In a few families the violence that occurred during pregnancy led to a miscarriage. It is possible that on a conscious
or subconscious level, violence toward a pregnant wife may
be a form of prenatal child abuse. Mrs. (80)'s comments give
at least some evidence to support this claim.

> Mrs. (80):    Oh yea, he hit me when I was pregnant. It was
> weird. Usually he just hit me in the face with his
> fist, but when I was pregnant he used to hit me in
> the belly. It was weird.

It may not have been just "weird," it may have been her
husband's attempt to terminate the pregnancy and relieve
himself of the impending stress that the new child would bring.

Other accounts of violence while the wife is pregnant reveal a variety of factors involved in the pregnancy. One wife reported that being pregnant made her irritable. She felt depressed by her having to be home and by her perceived lack of sexual attractiveness. Another wife discussed how she had become pregnant after trying for a long time, and her husband wondered whether or not he was the real father. In a third family, a wife got pregnant and this interfered with her husband's desire to go boating and water skiing.

It is impossible to come to a definitive conclusion about what causes the high association between pregnancy and family violence. A complex of stresses, strains, and frustrations apparently are involved in turning this period of family life into a crisis that can precipitate violent assaults on the pregnant woman.

### Sex and Family Violence

The family is the only legitimate outlet for sexual expression in our society (legal and social stigma are still attached to sex out of marriage despite the sexual revolution in our society). When one or both of the marital partners cannot fulfill the expectations concerning sexual expression and competence in the family, this can lead to a great deal of conflict. Frigidity, impotence, extramarital sex, jealousy, and arguments over sex were discussed by respondents in relation to outbreaks of conjugal brawls.

One of the most deadly verbal attacks a spouse can make is to attack the sexual ability or sexual flaws of the partner. Three wives discussed at length the verbal and physical battles that ensued after their husbands attacked them privately and publically for being "cold." Mrs. (48) was slapped and pushed by her husband on occasions when he complained that she was frigid.

Mrs. (48):     He used to tell everybody that I was cold. Of course he never bothered to explain that the reason I was,

was because he was always drinking, and I can't
stand drinking. Or that he was out all night long and
then when he came home he expected me to welcome him with open arms.

Mrs. (48)'s comments echo those from wives in Chapter 3
who resisted sleeping and having sex with their drunken
husbands. Their protests usually brought physical reprisal;
however, one wife was able to avoid sex by instigating a
physical fight. She was able to avoid having sex only if she
could get her husband to beat her, because he would hit her
and then leave the house for the night. Some husbands
needed little instigation, they would hit their wives simply
because they felt that their wives were frigid.

> Mrs. (18):  He was one of those who liked to strike out. He hit
> me and a lot of that was based on sex—he thought
> that I was a cold fish. I wasn't affectionate
> enough. . . . He'd come home and hit me and some-
> times he took a shotgun to me.

There are two sides to this coin. In three families, violent
incidents were precipitated by the wife's complaints that her
husband was not "aggressive enough." These wives complained that their husbands just didn't like sex. Whatever the
reason, the husband's apparent impotence was a major factor
involved in these occurrences of violence.

Other instances of sex-related violence were cases of husbands striking wives for suspected or detected infidelity or
wives striking husbands for the same reason. In a family cited
in Chapter 2, a wife hit her husband after he found out that
she was having an affair.

The intensity of family life is magnified in the tension,
frustration, and strain of sexual performance or sexual transgressions by the conjugal partners. Violent incidents stem-
ming from this context emanate from the core of both family
life and family stress.

## Structural Stresses Within the Family

There are indications that certain types of family structures produce high stress, which in some cases leads to conjugal violence. In particular, we were concerned as to whether size of the family or the religious differences between the spouses were in any way related to violent behavior.

*Number of Children.* Literature on child abuse reports that size of the family is related to abuse of children. Gil states that reported abuse is more common in families with four or more children (1971: 640). While violence towards children was found to be related to family size, we were interested as to whether family size also is related to conjugal violence. Table 22 shows no definitive relation between family size and conjugal violence.

The findings for parental violence and conjugal violence suggest that in some families, a large number of children can create financial, emotional, and psychological burdens for the parents and that this stress can lead to violence directed towards the source of the stress—the children—or between the husband and wife. Mrs. (32), who quarrels a great deal with her husband and who hits her children frequently, discussed the strain placed on her family life by too many children.

### TABLE 22
### CONJUGAL VIOLENCE BY NUMBER OF CHILDREN

| | Number of Children | | |
|---|---|---|---|
| | 0 - 2 (N=35) | 3 - 4 (N=31) | 5+ (N=14) |
| No Violence | 43% | 45% | 50% |
| Infrequent* Violence | 34 ⎱ 57 | 29 ⎱ 54 | 14 ⎱ 50 |
| Frequent** Violence | 23 ⎰ | 26 ⎰ | 36 ⎰ |

*from once in a marriage to six times a year
**from monthly to daily

Mrs. (32):    One problem was we lost our home. I had a mobile home and we got evicted because they said my kids broke windows and things. I went down to the office where they rented the homes and I said if they did any damage I would pay for it. They said that they couldn't prove anything. So we got evicted anyway and I had no place to put my trailer—with six kids—I had to give it back. And then I couldn't find an apartment because nobody around here wants six kids. I even tried in the city and that didn't work. Finally, my husband got talking to his boss and he got us here. I had six kids down staying with my sister and I didn't know what to do. So I said to my husband maybe it would be better if I went on some kind of aid or something. He said no. So finally I got up here—it worked out all right but I was really disgusted . . . I didn't really plan to have that many kids.

Other wives traced back their problems with their husbands and children to getting married too young and then to having too many children.

*Religion.* Earlier in this chapter it was shown that violence did not differ appreciably among different religious groups— with the exception of those individuals who had or gave no religious preference. However, looking within the family reveals that there is a much greater likelihood of violence occurring when there is a religious difference between the spouses (Table 23).

This finding is essentially similar to a finding in the study of child abuse that in four of seven cases of child abuse studied, women entered into marriage with men of different religions (Bennie and Sclare, 1969: 979). Again, we would propose that intermarriage can produce stress and conflict within the family that can lead to some form of intrafamily violence. In most cases of violence where there is religious difference, the actual difference does not directly lead to violence—rather the difference in religion contributes to arguments and conflict, which in turn becomes the foundation for future outbreaks of violence. In fact, many respondents gave the religious difference a low priority in their list of problems. The fact remains, however, that coming from different religious backgrounds and having different religious convictions is more likely to lead to stress, conflict, and violence than when the partners come from the same religious tradition.

*Stress.* In general, most violent families have their hands full coping with the tremendous stresses of family life. When they fail to cope, they frequently become violent. Some of the conflicts and arguments that lead to violence concern arguments over how to raise the children or money and finances, disputes with or over in-laws, gambling, and sometimes health problems of family members.

In addition to high stress leading to violence, we found a couple of families where low or no stress caused violence. In one particular instance, violence emerged out of boredom.

Mrs. (76):    I was a good housekeeper and mother, you know. I'd come that far. I socialized with my neighbors. We socialized with our neighbors. We got along fine—just him and me. But it was dull ... I was trying, you know. I probably had no reason to get angry with him ... but it was such a bore. I was trying to wake him up, you know. He was such a rotten lover anyway. So I'd yell at him and hit him to stir him up.

**TABLE 23**
**CONJUGAL VIOLENCE BY RELIGIOUS DIFFERENCE**

| | Religious Difference | |
| --- | --- | --- |
| | No Difference (N=50) | Religious Difference (N=30) |
| No Violence | 52% | 33% |
| Infrequent* Violence | 30 ⎫ 48 | 27 ⎫ 67 |
| Frequent** Violence | 18 ⎭ | 40 ⎭ |

*from once in a marriage to six times a year
**from monthly to daily

## SOCIAL STRUCTURE, FAMILY STRUCTURE, AND VIOLENCE: A LINKAGE

The analysis of families' position in the social structure and conjugal violence reveals that intrafamily violence, like other forms of violence (Coser, 1967: 55-57; Palmer, 1962: 34; Etzioni, 1971), is unevenly distributed in social structures. The examination of family structures of violent families illustrated that certain family structures produce more stress and frustration, which lead to violence. The linkage we posit is that the types of family structures that lead to violence are produced by these families' position in the social structure. Certain families, largely by their position in the social structure, suffer greater stress and frustration than do other families as a result of lack of resources and skills and because of certain structural arrangements within the family that tend to be associated with violence.

What emerges from the analysis of the violent family's position in society and the structure of the family is the fact that society's standards and expectations for role occupancy and behavior in the family often are at odds with certain individuals' abilities to fill these roles and meet the expectations. Society allocates roles, role obligations, and standards of performance for members of a family on the basis of sex and age (Goode, 1966). But society does not provide all these people with the desire, ability, tools, or resources with which to fill these roles. In addition, certain families suffer greater stress and frustration and often lack the resources to deal with or cope with these stresses. Additional children, health problems, unemployment, sexual difficulties, and other stressful events are much more problematic for families who do not have the material, emotional, psychological, or social resources to handle these events.

The conversations with the participants in family violence and the ensuing analysis of the data presents a persuasive argument for a structural approach to intrafamily violence. These preliminary foundations for a theory of intrafamily violence will be elaborated on, in detail, in the concluding chapter, where an integrated theory of intrafamily violence will be presented.

## NOTES

1. There are a number of studies that examine various aspects of family conflict, crisis, and disorder. Most of these focus on what Hill (1958: 142) called stressor events, which are either external to the family or within the family and how they affect family life. Cavan (1959) has studied the effects of unemployment on the family and how unemployment causes a strain on interpersonal roles when the husband cannot work and others usurp his role as wage earner. Rusk and Novey (1957) have examined the impact of chronic illness on the family. Bakan (1971) discusses how childbirth may lead to aggressive tendencies on the part of the wife. Three studies examine parenthood as family crisis (LeMasters, 1957; Dyer, 1963; Hobbs, 1965). Some researchers have focused on crisis and disorder caused by a disabled child (Dow, 1965) or a subnormal child (Schonell and Watts, 1956). Jackson (1958) has contributed a classic study on alcoholism and the family.

2. The data analysis in this section will be a simple cross-tabulation of specific independent variables such as education, occupational status, and income by the dependent variable—conjugal violence. There is the question of whether or not to run a control on this analysis for the source of the subject (that is, agency, agency neighbor, police, and police neighbor) because each group differs from the others in terms of both independent and dependent variables. It was decided *not* to run the control because the small sample size (N=80) would have meant dichotomizing the independent and dependent variables. This would have resulted in the loss of precision in the analysis and some valuable findings would have been lost.

3. For explanation of how occupational status was operationalized see Appendix A.

4. An important caveat that applies to this in discussion is that we have systematically excluded from our sample any "nonlegally" married couples. Therefore, we have no data on the occurrence and frequency of occurrence of violence between couples who are living together or who are engaged in a "trial marriage." Nevertheless, from our interviews we are still convinced that in most cases a marriage license also functions as a hitting license.

# Chapter 5

## "IT TAKES TWO":

## THE ROLES OF VICTIM AND OFFENDER

It was evident from conversations with members of violent families and from the discussions of conjugal violence that preceded this chapter that acts of intrafamily violence are not sporadic or patterned outbursts of irrational violence. Furthermore, the victims of these violent acts are not simply passive "hostility sponges" or "whipping boys" for their violent partners. On the contrary, the role of the victim in intrafamily violence is an important and active one. The actions of the victim are vital intervening events between the structural stresses that lead to violence and the violent acts themselves.

Some students of crime and violence have addressed themselves to the role of the victim in acts of violence. Hentig, in his work on the criminal and the victim, points out that in many cases the victim contributes to the genesis of the crime

(1948: 383). Schafer also proposes that the study of the criminal-victim relation, or what is often referred to as "victimology," is an integral part of the general crime problem (1968: 3). A major focus on the role of the victim in acts of violence is provided by Wolfgang's examination of victim-precipitated homicide. Wolfgang (1958: 252-254) found that the victim was a direct, positive precipitator of the crime in 26% of the criminal homicides documented in Philadelphia from 1948 to 1952. Palmer (1972) explains that violence often occurs after daily buildups of arguments and insults. Gil (1971) holds that some children play a provocative role in their behavior towards adults and this plays a contributing role in their own abuse.

A major finding in Wolfgang's research that applies to instances of family violence is that the male is the typical victim in cases of victim-precipitated homicide among family members. The usual course of events is that the husband lashes out and the wife responds in the extreme. When Wolfgang discusses victim precipitation he is referring to a situation where the victim, through his own actions, causes his own victimization. These precipitating actions can be the first use of violence, use of vile language (calling the offender a vile name), or infidelity (Wolfgang, 1958: 252). In some instances of victim-precipitated homicide, becoming the victim may be the result of a chance factor—someone's aim was poorer or he was not as quick to respond. In these cases, the victim, had things gone differently, might have been the slayer.

The role of the victim in conjugal violence, particularly nonlethal violence, which has been examined in this study, is not as physically provocative as it is in cases of homicide. While there were some families where the victim precipitated the violence by being violent, the majority of incidents of physical violence were caused by the victim's verbal behavior. As Hentig suggests, the usual role of the victim of intrafamily violence is one of tormentor (1948: 431).

This chapter examines the role of the victim by describing

typical actions that precipitate a physical attack. There are characteristic incidents that occur in family interaction that often lead to violence. Interfering with one partner's attempt to punish the children, nagging, arguments over drinking and gambling, using vile names, verbal criticisms of sexual performance, and escalating family arguments by bringing past and present conflicts into a fight all are part of the role of the victim in family violence. The first section summarizes material on the victim's role, which already has been discussed in earlier chapters. The following section on the response of the offender extends the analysis by theorizing how the victim's actions lead to the response of the offender. It is proposed that certain verbal assaults made by the victim, if directed at vulnerable aspects of the offender's self-concept, are likely to produce violent reactions. Moreover, the victim is able to direct these verbal salvos at the partner's vulnerable points because the intimacy and emotional closeness of marriage exposes each other's weaknesses (Goode, 1971: 632).

## THE ROLE OF THE VICTIM

### A Continuum of Provocation

The interviews with members of violent families gave the impression that the actions of victims that provoke violence from their spouses seem to be distributed along a continuum, ranging from actions that occasionally provoke violent responses to those which almost invariably lead to violence. On one extreme, verbal complaints by a wife or a husband sometimes can provoke a partner to violence, depending on the context and the amount of stress the partner is under at that particular time. However, verbal attacks are towards the middle on the continuum. These can be critical attacks that focus on a particular part of the other person's behavior or personality. They either can be aimed at one issue or they can escalate into a constellation of issues—past, present, and future. Finally, at the extreme on the continuum, where certain actions on the part of the victim almost always produce a violent response, there is physical violence on the part of the victim. In these instances, the victim is labeled "victim" because he or she received more violence or was injured.

*Nag, Nag, Nag.* When one thinks of victim-precipitated family violence, one often conjures up the image of the nagging wife who finally drives her husband to "belting her in the mouth." This image is fostered by countless stories told by stand-up comedians and scenarios played out on television situation comedies—for instance, Ralph Cramden on the old *Honeymooners* show threatens "one of these days . . . pow, right in the kisser."

There is a grain of truth in this image. Wives who have been hit or beaten by their husbands often explain that they provoked the attack by nagging their husbands.

Mrs. (45):  Well, I'm the first to admit that none of the wars would have started if I didn't provoke them. If I just kept my big mouth shut and come and go and let well enough alone, it never would have been anyway.

A number of the wives who were victims of conjugal violence felt that if they could have kept quiet, violence never would have occurred.

Mrs. (70):  I can't blame it all on me, but there are many times that I could have just shut my mouth—I'd keep at him and at him until he reached his breaking point.

Mrs. (75):  It wasn't too long ago. The baby was about 2 months old—July—we were fighting about something. I have a habit of not keeping my mouth shut. I keep at him and at him. He finally turned around and belted me. It was my fault, I asked for it.

It is a fallacy, however, to think that the wife is totally to blame and that she is a nagging shrew. In addition to admitting that they were nags, wives also explained that there was often a reason for their nagging. In Chapter 2, Mrs. (10) was hit in the eye by her husband after she kept asking him to help shovel the snow. Mrs. (51) admits that she nags her husband and this causes violence, but she also feels that he is "no angel either":

Mrs. (51):   He needed talking to by someone! It gets to be you live with a person for so long. And I'll admit, you can't always be nice—not when I'm working and keeping up so many children and the house. Course, he (her husband) didn't do a thing. In fact he was more trouble—in and out like a boy. I'd tell him sometimes, "You walk in like you want to. You've got a key. And yet there's no money being paid at the end of the week...." I'm sure I nagged, bothered, whatever you want to call it.

Mrs. (68) told of how she got sick of watching her husband sit around the house when she felt he ought to look for a job.

Mrs. (68):   If I were to aggravate him or bring up something, then he would get violent when he was drinking. But if he would come home and I would just leave him alone, no violence. But I just can't stand him half-asleep in that chair with no one for me to talk to—you want adult conversation.

Unfortunately, Mrs. (68) frequently got hit instead of conversation.

It is almost impossible in family interaction for a wife or a husband not to nag their spouse. As Mrs. (45) puts it, "You got to live in dead silence and then you don't have no fights." But, in most families, general nagging is less likely to produce a violent response than any other action by the victim. When

nagging does result in physical violence, the nagging and
ensuing violence is produced by an interaction of the frustrations of the wife, the frustrations of the husband, and the
contextual elements of the situation—in the privacy of the
home, no one present, time of day.

*Name Calling.* One step up from general nagging as an
action that leads to being hit is name calling, either in the
form of profanity or ethnic slurs. As with victim-precipitated
homicide (Wolfgang, 1958), the victim of conjugal violence
often causes his or her own victimization by calling the
spouse a vile name or directing a slur towards the spouse's
ethnicity. Mrs. (58), for instance, is incensed when her husband calls her names. Her response is a violent one.

> Mrs. (58):    Once in a while he'll say something to make me
>               mad—like he'll say, "You damn stupid Polak" . . . so
>               I punch him in the gut.

Mrs. (79) was hit repeatedly by her husband because in the
rage of an argument she would call him a bastard.

> Mrs. (79):    I had him arrested for assault and battery, you
>               know. We fought violently whenever we'd argue.
>               This is why I said he had his hangups about being
>               adopted. He claimed I called him a bastard or some-
>               thing. . . . Once he came after me with a knife.

*Verbal Attacks.* There are verbal attacks often made by
one spouse towards the other that are more specific than
simple or general nagging. These verbal blasts center on
specific traits or actions of the partner and are frequently
caused by and directed towards social, psychological, or
emotional "defects" in the partner. For instance, we saw
earlier that many wives are intensely upset by their husbands'
drinking or gambling. In other families, verbal attacks may be
directed at deficient sexual performance or sexual appetites
of the partner. Or, in an age of the "liberated woman," the

wife may attack her husband's "male chauvinist" attitude towards her. Verbal attacks also may emanate from the attacker's dissatisfaction with him or herself. Thus, the attacks of "male chauvinism" may arise from the wife's own dissatisfactions with being a "harried housewife."

Specific situations of verbal abuse provoked by the partner's drinking or sexual deficiencies have been cited earlier in Chapters 2, 3, and 4. Mrs. (45) seems to summarize these in a statement that reveals how her verbal attacks on her husband, prompted by his lack of sexual appetite, and his attacks on her for drinking led to *both* of them becoming victims of intrafamily violence.

> Mrs. (45): Well, let's put it this way. I don't know how to word it. Well, generally it's the man that's the (sexual) aggressor, and he's (her husband) not, you know . . . and before we'd fight over that. I think I understand him more, you know. I think I do. In the beginning he had the fear the children wouldn't be normal. That's what I feel. . . . Other times he called me an alcoholic, 'cause I drink . . . he calls me that. I like to drink, you know. I drink at night—a glass of beer—a couple of drinks. . . . When he calls me that it sets off the wars.

*The All-Out Verbal Attack.* Verbal attacks seldom confine themselves to one topic area. In our discussions with the victims of family violence, we discovered that the verbal assault that precipitated the violent assault was frequently multidimensional. Wives who are upset with their husbands' drinking often do not confine their complaints to that aspect of his behavior. In the section on "Alcohol and Violence" in Chapter 3, the wives' accounts of incidents of violence not only expressed their upset over their husbands' drinking but their anger over having to get up and cook for them and then have sex. They were extremely angry that their husbands had wasted the family income on liquor and gambling. With all this on their minds, their verbal assaults on their husbands consisted of multibarreled attacks on drinking, gambling, sexual demands, the family's poor financial state, and so on.

> Mrs. (18):    I'd get to telling him, "Why do you have to drink? Why do you have to play poker? Where are your responsibilities to me? If you want to spend money more than I do—just don't bother to pay the bills." And that would set him off.

The potential victim would begin with an attack on a current issue (drinking) and soon branch out into other areas, drawing from behavior and/or transgressions that had occurred or that might possibly occur in the future. The responses to these attacks were either other verbal attacks made by the partner, or violence.

These types of all-out fights are discussed by Bach and Wyden (1968) in their book, *The Intimate Enemy*. Bach and Wyden make the point that these multitopic verbal brawls are unfair and nonconstructive instances of family fighting. We found that the function of this type of verbal fighting in situations leading to violence is that the fights become so intense, and use ammunition from such a wide range of the marital partners' relationship, that they soon hit a nerve in one of the combatants and produce a violent retaliation. Physical violence is a response to the verbal assault that frequently ends the verbal abuse. It is possible that, in these cases, violence occurs when one of the partners is not able to compete with the other's verbal battering or runs out of verbal ammunition. In these instances, violence is a "resource" brought into play when verbal resources are insufficient.

*Violence to Violence.* It may confound the discussion to state that violence provokes violence, because the purpose of this section is to examine the role of the victim in precipitating violence. However, there are cases when the initial user of violence becomes the ultimate victim. Here the victim is the family member who is the most severely injured, even though he or she was the first to deploy physical violence.

The typical instance of violence provoking violence begins when the husband and wife are engaged in a verbal fight. At some point, as described in the previous section, one partner simply runs out of ammunition or patience and begins to flail away at the other. This, in turn, provokes a violent response and the ultimate victim is the partner who is hurt the most.

> Mrs. (52):   I don't remember what the fight was about, but I got so mad that I just didn't yell. Instead of yelling, I just swing and then he'll swing back. . . . And then I'd swing again, and he'd swing back and hit me hard enough so that I'd go into another room and just shut the door and that would be it.

The wife, however, is not the only victim in these instances of violence leading to violence. In fact, as Wolfgang (1958) discussed, the wife can respond to violence in the extreme and make her husband the injured victim.

> Mrs. (80):   He wants different things. Like if I'm there. They're not simple demands—like "clean the house" at 3 in the morning. If I don't do it he'll toss everything around. He threw lamps, sometimes tables at me. . . . I went after him with a knife once and I did it. . . . He went to the hospital and had to get sewed up.

In the cases of violence leading to violence, the determination of the ultimate victim may be influenced by such factors as who is stronger, who has the better aim, who has quicker access to a weapon, and so on. The main point is, that of the actions that lead to violence, the one which is probably the most likely to produce a violent response is violence itself.

## Summary

The continuum of provocation that has been described has not been developed with exact statistical evidence. There are no precise statistical data that verbal attacks are more likely to produce violence than name calling. The actual order of the actions of the victim in terms of likelihood of producing violence was generated by the qualitative analysis of the conversations with victims of violence. In particular instances of familial violence, the actions of the victim interacted with elements of the situation, the state of the offender, and the structure of the family. Certain people are able to withstand more verbal abuse than are others. In some families, a verbal attack might set off violence one time and be shrugged off another time.

The contribution the victim's role makes to the occurrence of violence cannot be evaluated in isolation from the other factors that have been discussed with regards to violence in the family. This discussion does provide some additional descriptive information about the dynamics of intrafamily violence.

## THE REACTION OF THE OFFENDER

There are two questions that need to be addressed in the analysis of the violent reaction of the offender to the actions of the victim. (1) Why are verbal assaults so devastating to the offender such that he or she retaliates violently? (2) What particular verbal salvos are most likely to provoke violent reactions?

The first question is answered by proposing that prolonged interaction, intimacy, and emotional closeness of family life expose the vulnerability of both partners and strip away the facades that might have been created to shield personal weaknesses of both husband and wife. As a result, couples become experts at attacking each other's weaknesses and are able to hurt each other effectively with attacks and counter-attacks (Goode, 1971: 632). Moreover, in the family, as opposed to other institutional or social settings, it is difficult to turn off verbal abuse by the most common method—not interacting with the person. In almost every setting for social interaction, individuals who want to avoid conflict or arguments can avoid interaction with potential antagonists. Husbands and wives find it difficult to do this.

The answer to the second question draws from the answer to the first, and posits that certain individuals have experienced self-devaluing experiences and thus, their self-evaluations are vulnerable. Gillen, for instance, describes murderers as characterized by a sense of inferiority (Gillen, 1946: 86). Given this vulnerability, one reaction to an attack or a perceived attack on an aspect of self-concept is violence towards the attacker.

## Intimacy and Vulnerability

Goode (1971) explained in his theoretical work on family violence, and we discovered in our interviews with the 80 families, that spouses, after living together for a few years, become experts as to their partner's vulnerability. Each soon learns what upsets the other. In the course of family squabbles, arguments, or confrontations, one or both of the spouses will "go for the jugular" by attacking weak spots. For instance, Mrs. (71) discovered that her husband gets upset because he does not seem to be able to handle their baby as effectively as she does. She uses this in the course of arguments.

Mrs. (71):   And I'll say, "But you can't take care of her (their baby)." If I want to hurt him I use that. We kind of use the baby now and it's really bad. I've tried to help so she won't feel that way towards him. He gets all nervous whenever she starts fussing. He'll just say, "Go to your mom" ... I throw it up to him that the baby is afraid of him when we argue.

Mr. (71) is able to retaliate with a verbal counterattack that he knows hurts his wife:

Mr. (71):   If I want to make her feel really bad, I tell her how stupid she is.

We repeatedly heard respondents tell stories of how they tried to cut down their spouses verbally and this eventually led to a physical assault.

Mrs. (70):    We were tearing each other down all the time. . . .
              He'd say things to just hurt me—how I clean the
              house. I'd complain about his work—he wasn't
              making enough money. . . . He'd get upset.

Mrs. (80):    I'd cut him down a bit . . . I figure it's the only way
              I can get back at him.

Mrs. (57):    If I really want to get him, I'll call him dirty names
              and he'll throw me down as trash.

## Vulnerability and Violence

In the chapters that preceded this discussion, and through-out this chapter, it becomes evident that particular things one partner will say often precipitate violence. The partner learns quickly what these incendiary topics are, and can use them or not depending on his or her perception of the situation. In terms of the offender who hears these attacks and responds violently, it appeared that the offender had some reason for being sensitive about certain issues—for instance, in some families calling a partner a bastard led to violence, in others it was criticisms of drinking and alcoholism, while in others it was attacks on sexual competence. Kaplan has proposed that aggressive individuals are more likely to have experienced self-devaluing experiences and their self-evaluations are vul-nerable (Kaplan, 1972: 602). Our conversations with re-spondents who were hit or have been hit by their spouse gave some indication that it was some previous psychosocial ex-perience that made their spouse highly vulnerable to attacks on his or her self-esteem. For instance, we cited the case of Mrs. (79) earlier, who got hit after calling her husband a bastard. Further conversations revealed that her husband was adopted as a child and had a great fear that he was illegiti-mate. Mrs. (61)'s husband, who hit her after she complained that he was not sexually aggressive enough, feared sex because his mother had a mental breakdown and he was afraid that if he had children they too would become "crazy." In other families, husbands who reacted violently to being called alcoholics had parents who were heavy drinkers or alcoholics.

It must be pointed out that violence is not the only response to an attack or perceived attack on a vulnerable aspect of an individual's self-concept. Verbal assaults on individuals with vulnerable self-esteem can result in verbal counterattacks, sarcasm, defensive posture, or withdrawal. This chapter has focused on only one of the possible reactions. Why a particular violent response is deployed by the offender requires a theoretical statement about the causes of intrafamily violence. The theoretical propositions on conjugal violence will be presented in the concluding chapter.

*Chapter 6*

## BASIC TRAINING FOR VIOLENCE

The family, more than any other social institution, is the primary mechanism for teaching norms, values, and techniques of violence. If we want to understand and explain violence (be it in the street or in the home), our attention ought to be directed towards the family more than, for example, to the effects of television violence on children (Larsen, 1968) or the impact of corporal punishment in the school. The empirical data (discussed in the following pages) on homicide, assault, child abuse, violent crimes, and violence between family members definitely tend to indicate that violent individuals grew up in violent families and were frequent victims of familial violence as children. The theoretical work on violence also points to the family as a major factor that contributes to violence by providing basic training for violence.

In our own research we found that many of the respondents who had committed acts of violence towards their spouses had been exposed to conjugal violence as children and had been frequent victims of parental violence. This exposure and experience often provided role models for the use of violence, and situations where accounting schemes were learned that justified and approved of violence. This chapter posits that the family serves as basic training for violence by exposing children to violence, by making them victims of violence, and by providing them with learning contexts for the commission of violent acts. Finally, the family inculcates children with normative and value systems that approve of the use of violence on family members in various situations.

## SOCIALIZATION AND VIOLENCE

A common factor throughout the research on violent individuals is that they had a high level of physical brutality inflicted on them throughout childhood and adolescence. Guttmacher's (1960) conclusion of a discussion about a group of murderers is that their common experience was the high level of violence inflicted on them by parents when they were growing up. Guttmacher (1960) states that this victimization produced a hostile identification by the victims (the eventual murderers) with their brutal aggressors and the murderers learned by conscious example that violence was a solution to frustration. Tanay's study of homicidal offenders finds that 67% had histories of violent child rearing (1969: 1252-1253). Palmer (1962) suspected that mothers of murderers were more aggressive towards them than their brothers. His data reveal that a slightly greater number of murderers than control brothers were beaten by their mothers (p. 76). In addition, fathers beat the murderers severely as opposed to control brothers (Palmer, 1962: 76). Palmer's later work on violence (1972) concludes that the early life histories of those who later commit homicides are characterized by extreme physical frustration (p. 53). In discussing a number of cases of homicide, Gillen (1946) cites murderers who received a high amount of physical punishment as children. In case #40, a father often beat his son when the boy was a child. The boy later goes on to kill his (the boy's) wife. Gillen concludes that murderers were more severely treated than other family members as children and that they were more severely treated than other types of prisoners (1946: 211). Leon's study of violent bandits in Colombia (1969) adds cross-cultural support to the relationship between violence received as a child and violence committed as an adult. Studying the childhood history of violent bandits, Leon observes that fathers of these bandits used brutal punishment in order to assert dominance over the family.

The literature on child abuse presents strong evidence that abusive parents were raised in the same style that they have re-created in the pattern of rearing their own children (Steele and Pollock, 1968: 111). Abused children are likely to become abusive adults (Bakan, 1971: 114; Kempe, 1962: 18; Gil, 1971: 641; Gelles, 1973).

Given the experience of violent individuals with violence when they were growing up, what is the mechanism that leads to them becoming violent adults? Theories and students of violence posit that the family serves as an agent of socialization in teaching violent behavior. Not only does the family expose individuals to violence and techniques of violence, the family teaches approval for the use of violence. Bakan asserts that every time a child is punished by violence he is being taught that violence is a proper mode of behavior (Bakan, 1971: 115). Goode (1971) concurs with this position by arguing that children are taught that violence is bad but shown by parents that violence can be used to serve one's own ends. Gold (1958) explains that modes of aggression vary among social classes as a result of different socialization experiences. These different socialization experiences are the different types of punishment meted out by parents of misbehaving children (p. 654). Where physical punishment is used (in the lower classes) it serves to identify this type of behavior as approved behavior when one is hurt or angry. The punishing parent serves as a model for aggressive behavior (Gold, 1958: 654).

Other theoretical and empirical work further emphasizes the position that the family plays a major role in teaching violent behavior and proviolent norms. Bandura, Ross, and Ross (1961) would assert that children viewing their parents' acts of violence towards each other might imitate this behavior as children and in later life. And Guttmacher cites the fact that a number of murderers observed violence in a parent (1960: 61). A study of exposure to violence and violence approval (Owens and Straus, 1973) reveals a high correlation between observation of and experience with violence as a child and violence approval. Another discussion of violence asserts along the same line that violence is learned through childhood experience with violence and viewing the parent as a role model of violence (Singer, 1971; Gelles, 1973). This approach proposes that interpersonal violence reflects the shared meanings and role expectations of the person and others with whom he interacts. Self-attitude theory (Kaplan, 1972), structural theory (Coser, 1967; Etzioni, 1971), and culture of violence theory (Wolfgang and Ferracuti, 1967) all state, to a greater or lesser degree, that patterns endorsing violent responses are transmitted to children in the course of parent-child interaction and day-to-day family life.

## EXPERIENCE WITH VIOLENCE

Based on the theoretical and empirical work on violence we expected to find that: first, respondents who had observed violence between their parents would engage in more conjugal violence as adults than respondents who had not observed violence between their parents; and second, respondents who had been victims of violence in childhood would be more likely to engage in conjugal violence as adults than individuals who had not been victims of childhood violence or who had been victimized less.

The respondents who had observed their parents engaging in physical violence were in fact much more likely to physically fight with their own spouses than the people we interviewed who never saw their parents physically fight (Table 24).

TABLE 24

**PERCENT OF RESPONDENTS WHO PHYSICALLY FOUGHT WITH SPOUSE BY RESPONDENT'S OBSERVATION OF CONJUGAL VIOLENCE IN FAMILY OF ORIENTATION**

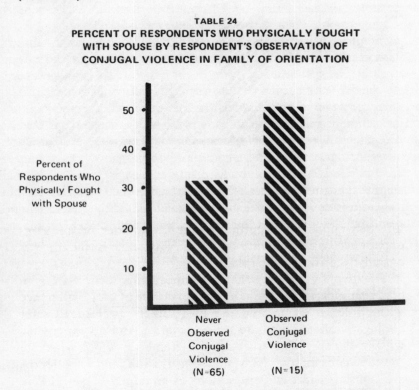

The data for victimization as a child and later violence with a spouse are not as clear-cut. Those respondents who had been frequent victims of violence as children were more likely to be violent toward their spouses than people who were never hit as children (Table 25). However, the individuals who were hit infrequently as children were *less* likely to

## TABLE 25
## PERCENT OF RESPONDENTS WHO PHYSICALLY FOUGHT
## WITH SPOUSE BY PARENTAL VIOLENCE TOWARD
## RESPONDENT AS CHILD

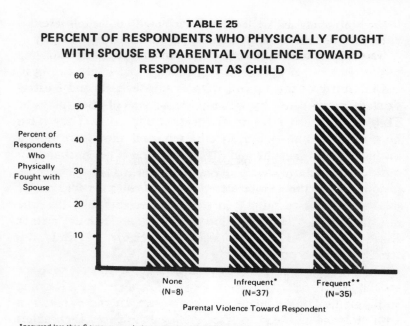

*occurred less than 6 times a year during respondent's childhood and adolescence
**occurred from monthly to daily during respondent's childhood and adolescence

hit their spouses than either the no-experience or frequent-experience with violence groups. Why this is the case is extremely difficult to explain.

The two hypotheses that introduced this section are generally supported by the data. Observation of and experience with violence as a child are more likely to lead to later conjugal violence than are no observation and no experience with violence.[1] The question still remains—why? What are the mechanisms by which these observations and experiences are translated into violent actions as an adult? Singer (1971: 31) provides the initial rationale for positing that these observations and experiences have a deep and lasting effect on eventual violent behavior towards family members:

In new situations where a child is at loss for what to do he is likely to remember what he saw his parents do and behave accordingly, even to his own detriment. Indeed, adults when they

become parents and are faced with the novelty of the role revert
to the type behavior they saw their parents engage in when they
were children sometimes against their current adult judgement.

Children growing up are witness to the trials and frustrations of married life by viewing the actions of their parents.
They see how to react to frustration and crisis. They learn
how to raise and to punish children, and they learn how a
husband treats his wife and how a wife treats her husband. In
our society, there are no other institutions that teach these
lessons (with the minor exception of the "preparation for
marriage" courses taught in some universities and the role
models presented by television family shows such as "Father
Knows Best," "The Dick Van Dyke Show," "All in the
Family," and so on).

Our conversations with the members of the 80 families
indicated that basic training for violence consists of a learning
situation that takes place where observation and experience
with violence can lead to later conjugal violence. Techniques
of violence, approval of violence, and accounting schemes for
violence all are learned in the family by seeing one's own
parents fight and by being struck as a child.

## LEARNING THE SCRIPT: TECHNIQUES, APPROVAL, ACCOUNTING SCHEMES OF VIOLENCE

The interviews yielded some important insights into the
process by which experience with violence leads to intrafamily violence. In many cases, these insights are drawn from
the discussions of how the respondent acts towards his or her
spouse and children and the discussions of life in the respondent's family of orientation. It was evident that many of the
techniques of intrafamily violence are passed on from generation to generation. Where one mother uses a belt on her
children, we found that she had been hit with a belt by her
parents. If a wife slaps her husband, she may have observed

her mother do the same thing to her father. Also, a very
strong theme in the interviews was how approval and justification for violence is taught. Many discussions of "normal
violence" between husband and wife and parents and children were followed later in the interview by the respondent
recalling a time when he was hit, or when his father hit his
mother, and how these incidents happened because the victim "deserved to be hit." Finally, there is the subtle teaching
of the entire script of intrafamily violence in the accounting
schemes that are learned. The homily of "sparing the rod and
spoiling the child," the justifications for violence, and the
whole approval of violence in the family comprised a detailed
accounting scheme which, for the respondents, explained
much of the violence that they either committed as adults or
were victims of in their childhood.

## Techniques of Violence

Although there were some discussions of techniques of
conjugal violence learned from observing or experiencing
violence in the family, the most lucid discussions came when
the topic was how one behaved towards his own child and
how he was treated by his own parents. Individuals learn
much about how to be physically violent by being hit or
watching someone else being hit. First, the particular
methods and instruments of violence are learned. Whether
an individual uses his hand, a belt, a curtain rod, or a
yardstick is greatly determined by how he was hit as a child
and what techniques were deployed by his parents on each
other and on the other children. When respondents stated
how they hit their children and then, later in the conversation, discussed how they were treated by their parents, the
instruments were sometimes identical. It must be pointed out
that these discussions were not connected and occurred at
completely different times in the conversation. In addition,
the interviewers never referred to what the respondent said
previously about how he punished his child when the discussion concerned how he was punished as a child. For example,

Mrs. (2) first discussed how she punishes her children. Later, she talked about the types punishment she received.

> Mrs. (2): I rant and rave and sometimes I get my yardstick. Sometimes if they are close I haul off with my hand. But they are getting so big that it's too painful.

> Interviewer: What kind of punishment or discipline would your parents let out to you?

> Mrs. (2): We usually got the yardstick.

Some respondents made the connection that they used the same method to raise their children that their parents used on them.

> Mrs. (20): I guess she punished us the same way I do my kids—with probably a belt or do without things.

In addition to teaching the use of particular instruments, the family also teaches *why* an instrument or technique is deployed. In Mrs. (47)'s family the instrument was not as important as its impact—it had to sting to be effective.

> Mrs. (47): I used to spank them. I used to have, you know, those yardsticks. Of course, they're not really heavy or anything, but they sting, you know.

When she talked about how she was punished she said:

> Mrs. (47): I think that's the only time he used a razor strap on me. The other times we had to go out and pick our own peach tree switch, you know, because they're very strong and they sting like mad!

The learning of techniques of violence also applies to learning *when* to employ these techniques. In Chapter 2 we talked about a calculus that parents develop to determine when and where to use force and violence. These calculi are often learned from one's own parents and by using one's own childhood as a guideline. Mr. (42) gets upset by his children's talking back. When they do this they get a slap in the mouth:

Mr. (42):   They talk back—that gets me upset. . . . One of them talked back to me once, about three years ago and I hit him in the mouth.

To understand why Mr. (42) gets upset when his children talk back and why they get slapped in the mouth for this, we can examine Mr. (42)'s experience as a child.

Mr. (42):   I never got a spanking. I can remember talking back to my mother once—my father never hit us. I can remember my mother giving me a belt in the mouth. That was the only time I ever talked back to my mother.

The accounts of the respondents add further evidence to the assertion made in the research of Bandura and his colleagues on imitative and modeling behavior, which show that children and young adults imitate the behavior of aggressive models (Bandura, Ross, and Ross, 1961). For those who are less than convinced that role models do lead to imitation, there is the story told by Mrs. (10):

Mrs. (10):   My daughter would sit down with a little blanket she had and she would put it between her legs and she would say that daddy hit mother like this and she would bang on the blanket, you know.

Individuals not only imitate in later life the behavior they witnessed as children, they also learn how to hit, what to hit with, what the impact should be, and what the appropriate circumstances are for violence.

## Approval of Violence

A recent analysis of data from a national survey conducted in 1968 for the President's Commission on the Causes and Prevention of Violence revealed that approval of inter- personal violence is highly related to experiencing violence as a child (Owens and Straus, 1972: 13). Our interview data confirm this finding and demonstrate that observing violence and being a victim of violence as a child can lead to approval of the use of interpersonal violence among family members. Mrs. (75), who has been hit by her husband, learned as a child that sometimes a wife deserves to be hit.

> Mrs. (75):   My father spanked my mother when I was about 5 years old. I don't know what it was for, but I know my mother told me father spanked her. That's the only time he ever laid a hand on her—she must have done something to deserve a spanking.

Being a victim of violence also contributes to an "I de- served it" outlook, which leads to approval of the use of interpersonal violence in the family.

> Mrs. (1):   The only time my father ever hit is when I swore at my mother. And I deserved it, you know. He slapped me across the mouth when he was really mad. You know, I deserved to be hit, I realized that.

> Mrs. (27):   Well, it didn't happen often, but the spankings I got I remembered and I think that helped. I think it really depends on the child—like with me, a spank- ing helped—very rarely did I get one. . . . My father used a strap. It sounds terrible—it sounds terrible because we had it very easy. He used to take the end of the strap and give us a crack across the fanny— but it was never anything to leave a mark. When you think of a barber belt there is a line in it. And you think, my God, what a thing to hit a child with. But he never whipped us with it—and it helped.

Thus, our respondents provide a vivid demonstration of how observation and experience with violence as a child can be translated into violence approval as an adult.

## Violence and Accounting Schemes

A major problem in positing that experience with violence leads to approval of violence is that this does not necessarily mean that it causes violent actions. As most students of attitudes and behavior know, there is no one-to-one relationship between attitudes toward a particular behavior and engaging in that behavior. Thus, if an individual approves of violence, he may not necessarily engage in a violent act towards a family member. We would argue, however, that a plausible sequence is that approval of violence contributes to the development of an accounting scheme that family members can use to explain or justify incidents of intrafamily violence. Moreover, the existence of this accounting scheme may facilitate violent behavior by providing, in advance, acceptable accounts that serve to justify the behavior despite cultural prescriptions and proscriptions about intrafamily violence. An example of an accounting scheme for parental violence that has been passed down for three generations and is now being taught to a fourth, is given by Mrs. (19):

Mrs. (19):   The rules were set and they were to be followed. If I did something wrong I was given a beating right on the spot. My mother was a church-going woman. She went to church. She'd say I don't have time, but when I come back I'm going to hunt you down and spank you. We got it right then and there—right on the nose because that was the promise she made. I also believe that when I'm raising my children—I should be a little more lenient—but with my leniency I also believe that when I tell my girls to be home at a certain time, I expect that. But see then too, I also raised my children on faith and trust which I guarantee this from every mother and father. I really do. I never had much education and I don't believe in reading out of books or this sort of

> thing because I wasn't raised up on no book. I just
> believe in knowledge. I love my children. I raised
> them and even my little grandchild—when I see her
> doing something wrong I'm going to spank her. I
> mean it's as simple as that, you know.

Mrs. (19)'s point may be well taken, it could be as simple as that. The more violence one is exposed to in childhood, the more one learns violence. At the same time, one also learns violence approval. If an individual has an accounting scheme that rationalizes and justifies violence, then this can lead to deploying those violent acts as an adult that were learned as a child.

## VIOLENCE AS LEARNED BEHAVIOR

The conclusion of this discussion is that violence is learned behavior. We have been asserting that violence, and violence towards family members in particular, is learned by experiencing violence while growing up in a family. Where an individual experiences violence as a child he is more likely to engage in violence as an adult.

> Mrs. (48):    He's (her husband) very rough. Always pushing me
> around. You know, not hitting, you know, but just
> putting his hand against me and just shoving or stuff
> like grabbing. I was always black and blue from
> where he grabbed me. He was this way. He never
> knew anything gentle. He was very, very rough and
> this was the way he handled everything. And it
> wasn't something, you know, he didn't always do it
> out of temper most of the time. He did it because
> this was what he learned. He never knew any
> different.

When individuals do not experience violence in their families as they are growing up, they are less likely to be violent adults.

Mr. (60):     We're not trying to impress you how good a family
              we are or our parents were. It is just like I told you
              at the beginning—the way we were brought up—we
              just weren't brought up in violence.

We have stated that the more violence is present in the
family, the more a person learns violence. In the concluding
chapter we will propose that violence is more common in
certain social structures. Families in these positions are more
violence-prone because, first, certain structural arrangements
that are common in these families lead to violence; and
second, as Coser (1967) has stated, violence is learned in
some social structures more than in others.

## NOTES

1. We will use these findings in this chapter to argue a socialization
approach to violence. However, these findings also are consistent with a
genetic theory of violence because the association between violence
experienced and observed in one's family of orientation and conjugal
violence in the family of procreation could arise out of genetic factors—
that is, violent individuals inherited genes that produced violence in
both generations.

# Chapter 7

# A SOCIAL STRUCTURE OF VIOLENCE

The research that we have reported on was undertaken in order to narrow existing gaps in the systematic knowledge concerning the extent and nature of violence between husbands and wives. It is well recognized among police, lawyers, and students of interpersonal violence that violence in the family is extremely common. Even though there is an appreciation for how extensive family violence is, we lack data concerning the incidence of physical violence between spouses. In addition, although these professional groups are aware of the extent of family violence, they tend to compartmentalize this knowledge in a way that denies the pervasive nature of the phenomenon. For example, the widespread knowledge of the frequency of murder between family members is not usually taken as an indication of a much higher frequency of nonlethal violence. Furthermore, when nonlethal violence between family members is considered, it tends to be thought of as a characteristic of the poor, mentally ill, and other deviant groups (Steinmetz and Straus, 1974).

The interviews with the 80 family members revealed that

violence had occurred in 55 percent of the families. More-over, in 26 percent of the entire sample, conjugal violence was a regular occurrence, ranging from a dozen times a year to daily. Although the sampling of families was not intended to be representative of any population, our interviews with the neighbors of police and agency families evidenced a high level of conjugal violence within families in which there was no public knowledge of violence. Therefore, we conclude that conjugal combat is extensive and that much of this violence is patterned and regular rather than isolated incidents.

The major value of the research, beyond positing a rough estimate of the incidence of family violence, lies in the examination and explication of the various dynamics of family violence and rate differentials of family violence across the social structure. We have analyzed the violent situation, the location of violent families in the social struc-ture, the dynamics of violent families, the factors that are associated with violence—such as pregnancy and social isolation—the roles of victim and offender, and the mecha-nisms by which the family serves as basic training for vio-lence. This analysis has indicated that intrafamily violence is a multidimensional phenomenon. We conclude this investiga-tion of conjugal combat by examining the relationship be-tween the factors that are associated with intrafamily violence. In the next section, this is accomplished through the use of a block diagram. The following section proposes an integrated theory of family violence that is generated from existing theories of violence and from the data gathered in this research. The chapter concludes with an evaluation of our current knowledge of family violence and prospects for future work on this topic.

## A MODEL OF CONJUGAL VIOLENCE

Clearly, there are multiple factors involved in conjugal violence. It is difficult to conceive of violent acts between family members as arising out of a single causal factor, such as a psychopathic or genetic condition, because of the various social and social psychological elements that are associated with occurrences and patterns of family violence. In order to provide a systematic overview of the elements that are related to violence between family members, we have developed a "block diagram" model. The diagram includes only those aspects of conjugal violence that have been dealt with in this research. As such, the diagram cannot be considered logically complete because it does not consider factors that, because of the design and nature of the data gathered, were not examined in the research (such as certain individual characteristics of family members—personality traits, psychopathological traits; the types of family lives that aggressive individuals experienced that may be associated with later violence—dominant mother, unsatisfactory experiences with father; or the total meaning of violence for the entire family).

Considering the factors that were discussed in the previous chapters on conjugal violence, we can conceptualize family violence in terms of a model such as the one presented in Figure 2. This model assumes that family violence is a function of two major conditions. First, violence is an adaptation or response to structural stress. Structural stress produces frustration, which is often followed by violence (expressive violence). Structural stress also produces role expectations (particularly for the husband) which, because of lack of resources, only can be carried out by means of violence (instrumental violence). The second major precondition for violence is socialization experience (bottom path of the diagram). There are a variety of responses to stress (Merton, 1938). If an individual learns that violence is an appropriate behavior when one is frustrated or angry, punishing his children, or arguing with his wife, then this will be the adaptation to stress deployed.

The situational context is a major intervening variable in the causal sequence that leads to violence. Certain situations are less prone to violence than others—out of the home, bystanders present, available avenues of escape from conflict.

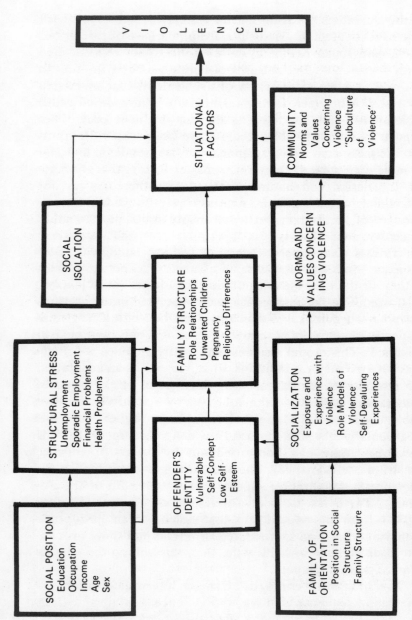

**Figure 2. A MODEL OF INTRAFAMILY VIOLENCE**

Other contexts are more likely to lead to violence—no avenues of escape, no nonfamily members present, arguments over alcohol or sex, precipitating actions by the victim.

Other factors that have been discussed in relation to family violence are social isolation and the offender's identity. We found that violent families are characterized by isolation from their neighbors. This seemed to leave them cut off from social resources. The lack of social support may contribute to an escalation of family problems, stress, conflict, and ultimately to violence. A pervasive theme in the interviews was that violence in the family often arose out of threats to the offender's identity. While we were not able to gather sufficient data to provide an in-depth analysis of this aspect of violence, we posited that certain social psychological experiences that offenders underwent as children, adolescents, and adults resulted in a vulnerable self-concept or a devalued sense of self. This contributed to the offender's feeling particularly threatened by challenges or perceived challenges to his or her position in the family. The offender's low sense of self-esteem has a large impact on family structure and family interaction and can be an incendiary factor in escalating family conflict into violence.

The nature of physical violence in the family is also a complex phenomenon. Violence can be a one-time outbreak in a marriage or it can be a weekly or even a daily affair. The victims and offenders may be the same family members for all occurrences of violence, or each incident may produce a different aggressor and victim. In explaining these different modes of family violence, one needs to trace the level and nature of stress, the socialization experiences of the participants, and examine the variable situational contexts of violence.

## A SOCIAL STRUCTURAL THEORY OF VIOLENCE

We stated that a major goal of this research was to develop a more adequate theoretical understanding of violence between family members. Towards this end, we synthesized the approaches offered by theories of violence (Straus, Gelles, Steinmetz, 1973) and attempted to examine the postulates presented in light of the data gathered in this research. In concluding, we offer an integrated theory of conjugal violence. The theory is "integrated" in the sense that it "grounds" (Glaser and Strauss, 1965) the existing theoretical conceptualizations of violence in the data gathered on conjugal violence.

An implicit theme in the presentation of the research on conjugal violence is that the findings of the study are most consistent with a *social structural theory of violence*. We have found, in the study of 80 families, that violence is more likely to occur in families located on the lower rungs of the social ladder. In addition, there are certain patterned role relations and contextual circumstances that take place in families, which frequently lead to violence. The theory of a social structure of violence has been presented in the work of Coser (1967), Etzioni (1971), Kaplan (1972), Gold (1958), and Owens and Straus (1973). These presentations served as the starting point for the theoretical conceptualization of family violence. In addition, some elaboration of the empirical parameters and dynamics of violence has been achieved through the use of the block diagram in Figure 2. We develop the structural theory of family violence more fully in the 5 propositions that follow. The use of these propositions is not intended as a formal proof, but only as a device for making the nature of the argument explicit.

### The Propositions

1. *Violence is a response to particular structural and situational stimuli.* In the interviews with members of violent families we found few cases where violence was an "irrational attack." Generally, violence is a response to stress and frustration or to threats to identity. There are particular family structures, such as where the husband has less education and occupational prestige than his wife or when the husband and

wife come from different religious traditions, and particular stressful situations, such as unemployment, unwanted or undesirable pregnancy, which lead to violence.

2. *Stress is differentially distributed in social structures.* Those families that have less education, occupational status, and income are *more likely* to encounter stressful events and have stressful family relations then are families with higher education, occupational status, and income. In addition, the ability to cope with the stress is unevenly distributed. Consequently, families that encounter the most stress have the fewest resources to cope with it.

3. *Exposure to and experience with violence as a child teaches the child that violence is a response to structural and situational stimuli.* The role models for violence presented to an individual in his childhood provide a learning situation where the use, rationale, and approval of violence are learned. Having a role model of violence can create a preference for violent responses to the stimuli as opposed to other responses—withdrawal, suicide, "psychological" violence.

4. *Individuals in different social positions are differentially exposed both to learning situations of violence as a child and to structural and situational stimuli for which violence is a response as an adult.* This proposition draws from Propositions 2 and 3. It asserts that certain individuals, as a result of their social position, will have been socialized to the use of violence in certain situations. As a result of being located in these social positions, individuals also are more likely to be exposed to these situations where violence is an appropriate reaction. This is a result of the differential distribution of norms that approves of violence and the causes of violence in social structures.

5. *Individuals will use violence towards family members differently as a result of learning experience and structural causal factors that lead to violence.* Family violence generally is explained by examining the factors in society and the family that lead to violence and whether or not an individual learns to use violence in these situations.

## A Theory of Intrafamily Violence

Although the theoretical propositions presented in the previous section were drawn from data that deal solely with nonlethal conjugal violence, we would further posit that this theoretical conceptualization is applicable to other forms of family violence, particularly violence by parents towards their children and lethal family violence. A similar model to Figure 2 has been presented elsewhere (Gelles, 1973) to account for child abuse. The data and research on child abuse suggest that violence toward children is largely determined by the family's position in the social structure, structural stress, and socialization to violence (Gil, 1971; Gelles, 1973). The theory also can be applied to incidents of homicide in the family because, as Pittman and Handy (1964) and Pokorny (1965) argue, the difference between homicide and assault is one of degree of violence and not kind.

It should not be construed that this presentation of a theory of intrafamily violence is at odds with all other theoretical positions. The propositions presented generally are consistent with, rather than contrasted to other theories of violence. The theory assumes much of the position of frustration-aggression theory, learning theory, self-attitude theory, and resource theory of violence (Straus, Gelles, Steinmetz, 1973). In terms of cultural theory of violence, our position is that norms and values that approve of violence and lead to a "subculture of violence" arise from the underlying social structure.

## CONCLUSION

This research has been an exploratory study of conjugal violence, and as such, we are not about to close the book on this subject based on interviews with 80, nonrandomly selected families. There are a number of liabilities with this work just as there are a number of assets. Furthermore, there are some issues that remain open and consequently we feel that there is still much work to be done in this area.

The major liability of the study is the sampling technique and the resulting sample. In no way are the 80 individual family members we talked to representative of any population. One-half of the sample was chosen because we knew in advance that there was a high likelihood of violence occurring between husband and wife. The other half of the sample, the neighbors, consists of individuals who were home during the hours we were in the neighborhood, and who consented to be interviewed. Third, the subjects are mostly wives and thus, their perspective and biases are reflected in much of what we have said about violence and the meanings of violence. Because of the nature of the sample, great care must be taken in inferring that the incidence data reported on violence are applicable to any population other than the 80 individuals interviewed. While *we* remain convinced that family violence is common in society, and our convictions were bolstered by the incidence of conjugal violence reported on the neighbor families, the incidence data in no way can be logically generalized to any other population, be it local or national.

A second problem with the research is that the small sample size inhibited full statistical testing of the quantitative data. Consequently, there is a problem inferring whether or not the relationships we found are, in fact, true associations or are occurring because of random factors. The findings reported and the conclusions suggested in this research require fuller, more rigorous testing and support.

There are a number of strengths of this research. First, this is a unique study. The area of conjugal violence has long remained an unrecognized and unresearched aspect of family life. Although our sampling method precludes much generalization, we were able to gain an insight into the dynamics of intrafamily violence by concentrating our efforts on interviewing families where we knew in advance that violence had occurred. The informal interview technique produced a wealth of data, which are characterized by their richness and detail. Second, although the findings remain to be confirmed in future research with a larger sample size and more rigorous analysis, the data reported here are largely consistent with other research on violence and violence between family members.

There are some aspects of conjugal violence where tentative conclusions have been reached. In the first place, this project proves that it is possible to undertake such research. This was a real concern in our design stage, as we were uncertain as to whether or not people would be willing to talk freely about violence in the family. Second, violence between family members is extensive. Neither the 57% violent figure for the entire sample nor the 37% violent figure for neighbor families can serve as definitive estimates of the extent of family violence in society. But taking into account the figures on the extent of conjugal violence given in other studies (Levinger, 1966; O'Brien, 1971), we estimate that violence is indeed common in American families. Furthermore, these incidents of violence are not isolated attacks nor are they just pushes and shoves. In many families, violence is patterned and regular and often results in broken bones and sutured cuts. Finally, while violence occurs in families at all socioeconomic levels, it is most common in families occupying positions at the bottom of the social structure. Clinical and newspaper reports of family violence make special efforts to point out the cases where conjugal violence occurs in homes of professional men (see, for example, *Newsweek*, 1973b: 39). In fact, in our own research, one of the more violent families was the family that had the highest total income in the entire sample. However, the bulk of conjugal violence and violence towards children occurs in families with low income, low educational achievement, and where the husband has low occupational status.

It is hoped that future research on family violence might take some of the findings and ideas presented in this study and employ them as a basis for intensive investigations. Longitudinal studies of violence in the family would contribute to an understanding of how violence evolves in the life patterns of families. Other examinations might focus on the relationship between forms of intrafamily violence—is conjugal violence somehow related to violence towards children or are they mutually exclusive in the same family? We are still at a loss to explain why beatings during pregnancy are so common. Finally, there is the question as to why men and women who are beaten by their spouses stay married. We feel that research on "threshholds of violence," which would locate at what point people will call for intervention in violence or dissolve a violent family, is quite important for a full understanding of the dynamics of family violence.

With all the discussion of data and the quotes from the interviews, and given whatever scholarly and heuristic value this research holds, there is one element of investigation that has been given especially little attention here. Throughout the interviewing and later during the analysis of the interviews, the most pervasive theme that we encountered was the pathos of violence in the family. Many men and women who were victims of violence usually were completely at a loss as to what to do. They pondered divorce but feared that this would lead to further attacks. They sometimes tried to gain police or court intervention, but that gave only temporary relief. On the other side of the coin, those offenders we talked to struggled hard to justify their actions, but often simply confessed that they hit their spouse or child because they could not help themselves or that they knew of no other way to handle the situation.

The extent of conjugal violence and the intensity of the pathos caused by family violence indicate that violence between family members is a social problem of major proportions. This problem mandates concentrated effort on the part of social work agencies, legislative bodies, and researchers to recognize, study, and provide appropriate services for families. This type of approach already has begun in the area of child abuse with large allocations of funds for studying the causes and means of preventing violence towards children. It is hoped that this research will provide one beginning toward a concentrated effort on preventing conjugal violence.

# REFERENCES

ADELSON, L. (1972) "The battering child." Journal of the American Medical Association 22 (October 9): 422-430.

BACH, G. R. and P. WYDEN (1968) The Intimate Enemy. New York: Avon Books.

——— (1969) "Art of family fighting." New York Times (January 26): 61-62ff.

BAKAN, D. (1971) Slaughter of the Innocents: A Study of the Battered Child Phenomenon. Boston: Beacon Press.

BALES, R. F. (1950) Interaction Process Analysis: A Method for the Study of Small Groups. Reading, Mass.: Addison-Wesley.

BANDURA, A., D. ROSS, and S. ROSS (1961) "Transmission of aggression through imitation of aggressive models." Journal of Abnormal and Social Psychology 63 (3): 575-582.

BANDURA, A. and R. W. WALTERS (1963) Social Learning and Personality Development. New York: Holt, Rinehart & Winston.

BECKER, S. (1963) Outsiders: Studies in the Sociology of Deviance. New York: Free Press.

BENNIE, E. H. and A. B. SCLARE (1969) "The battered child syndrome." American Journal of Psychiatry 125 (July): 975-978.

BERKOWITZ, L. (1962) Aggression: A Social Psychological Analysis. New York: McGraw-Hill.

BETTELHEIM, B. (1967) "Children should learn about violence." Saturday Evening Post 240 (March 11): 10-12.

BINFORD, S. (1972) "Apes and original sin." Human Behavior 1 (November/December): 65-71.

BLUMBERG, M. (1964) "When parents hit out." Twentieth Century 173 (Winter): 39-44.

BOSSARD, J. H. S. and E. S. BOLL (1966) The Sociology of Child Development. New York: Harper & Row.

Boston Globe (1972) "Chicago boy dies from parent beating." (September 1): 38.

——— (1972) "Southend woman, son shot in apartment." (September 1): 38.

——— (1973) "Home strife number one cause of murders in Atlanta." (February 6): 12.

BOUDOURIS, J. (1971) "Homicide and the family." Journal of Marriage and the Family 33 (November): 667-682.

BROWN, C. (1965) Manchild in the Promised Land. New York: New

American Library. (Pp. 263-271 reprinted as "The family and the subculture of violence," in Suzanne K. Steinmetz and Murray A. Straus [eds.] Violence in the Family. New York: Dodd, Mead 1974.)

BRYANT, C. D. and J. G. WELLS (1973) Deviancy and the Family. Philadelphia: F. A. Davis Co.

BUCKLEY, W. (1967) Sociology and Modern Systems Theory. Englewood Cliffs, N.J.: Prentice-Hall.

BURGESS, A. (1962) A Clockwork Orange. New York: Ballantine Books.

CAVAN, R. S. (1959) "Unemployment—crisis of the common man." Marriage and Family Living 21 (May): 139-146.

COHEN, A. K. (1955) Delinquent Boys: The Culture of the Gang. New York: Free Press.

COLES, R. (1964) "Terror-struck children." New Republic 150 (May 30): 11-13.

CORNING, P. A. and C. H. CORNING (1972) "Toward a general theory of violent aggression." Social Science Information 11 (June/August): 7-35.

COSER, L. A. (1967) Continuities in the Study of Social Conflict. New York: Free Press.

COURT-BROWN, W. M. (1967) Human Population Cytogenetics. New York: John Wiley.

CUBER, J. F. and P. B. HARROFF (1966) Sex and the Significant Americans. Baltimore: Penguin Books.

DAVIS, F. (1961) "Deviance disavowal: the management of strained interaction by the visibly handicapped." Social Problems 9 (Fall): 120-132.

DOLLARD, J. C., L. DOOB, N. MILLER, O. MOWRER, and R. SEARS (1939) Frustration and Aggression. New Haven: Yale University Press.

DOW, T. E., Jr. (1965) "Family reaction to crisis." Journal of Marriage and the Family 27 (August): 363-366.

DURKHEIM, E. (1951) Suicide: A Study in Sociology. Translated by John A. Spaulding and George Simpson. New York: Free Press.

DYER, E. D. (1963) "Parenthood as crisis: a re-study." Marriage and Family Living 25 (May): 196-201.

ELMER, E. et al. (1967) Children in Jeopardy: A Study of Abused Minors and Their Families. Pittsburgh: University of Pittsburgh Press.

ERON, L. D., L. O. WALDER, and M. M. LEFKOWITZ (1971) Learning of Aggression in Children. Boston: Little, Brown & Co.

ETZIONI, A. (1971) "Violence," pp. 709-741 in Robert K. Merten and Robert Nisbet [eds.] Contemporary Social Problems. 3rd ed. New York: Harcourt Brace Jovanovich.

FARBER, B. (1959) "Effects of a severely mentally retarded child on the family." Monographs of the Society for Research in Child Development 24 (No. 2).

FARBEROW, N. L. (1966) Taboo Topics. New York: Atherton Press.

FAULKNER, R. R. (1971) "Violence, camaraderie, and occupational character in hockey." Mimeo.

FREUD, S. (1920) A General Introduction to Psychoanalysis. Garden City, N.Y.: Garden City Publishing Co.

GALDSTON, R. (1965) "Observations of children who have been physically abused by their parents." American Journal of Psychiatry 122 (4): 440-443.

GELLES, R. J. (1973) "Child abuse as psychopathology: a sociological critique and reformulation." American Journal of Orthopsychiatry, 45 (July): 611-621.

GERTH, H. and C. W. MILLS (1953) Character and Social Structure: The Psychology of Social Institutions. New York: Harcourt Brace.

GIL, D. G. (1971) "Violence against children." Journal of Marriage and the Family 33 (November): 637-648.

GILLEN, J. L. (1946) The Wisconsin Prisoner: Studies in Crimogenesis. Madison: University of Wisconsin Press.

GIOVANNONI, J. (1971) "Parental mistreatment: perpetrators and victims." Journal of Marriage and the Family 33 (November): 649-657.

GLASER, B. G. and A. L. STRAUSS (1965) The Discovery of Grounded Theory: Strategies for Qualitative Research. Chicago: Aldine.

GOFFMAN, E. (1959) The Presentation of Self in Everyday Life. Garden City, N.Y.: Anchor Books.

GOLD, M. (1958) "Suicide, homicide and the socialization of aggression." American Journal of Sociology 63 (May): 651-661.

GOODE, W. J. (1966) "A theory of role strain," pp. 372-382 in Carl W. Blackman and Paul F. Secord [eds.] Problems in Social Psychology. New York: McGraw-Hill.

――― (1971) "Force and violence in the family." Journal of Marriage and the Family 33 (November): 624-636.

GRIBBON, A. (1972) "The war of the spouses: America's most hushed-up crime." National Observer (March 11).

GUTTMACHER, M. (1960) The Mind of the Murderer. New York: Farrar, Straus, and Cudahy.

HALL, O. (1948) "The stages in a medical career." American Journal of Sociology 53 (March): 327-336.

HELFER, R. E. and C. H. KEMPE [eds.] (1968) The Battered Child. Chicago: University of Chicago Press.

HENRY, A. F. and J. F. SHORT, Jr. (1954) Suicide and Homicide. New York: Free Press.

HENTIG, H. von (1948) The Criminal and His Victim: Studies in the Socio-biology of Crime. New Haven: Yale University Press.

HESS, R. D. and G. HANDEL (1959) Family Worlds. Chicago: University of Chicago Press.

HILL, R. (1949) Families Under Stress. New York: Harper.

——— (1958) "Social stresses on the family." Social Casework 39 (February/March): 139-150.

HOBBS, D. F., Jr. (1965) "Parenthood as crisis: a third study." Journal of Marriage and the Family 27 (August): 367-372.

HUMPHREYS, L. (1970) Tearoom Trade: Impersonal Sex in Public Places. Chicago: Aldine.

JACKSON, J. K. (1958) "Alcoholism and the family." Annals of the American Academy of Political and Social Science 315 (January): 90-98.

JAMES, W. T. (1951) "Social organization among dogs of different temperament: terriers and beagles reared together." Journal of Comparative Physiological Psychology 44: 71-77.

JOHNSON, R. N. (1972) Aggression in Man and Animals. Philadelphia: W. B. Saunders Co.

KAPLAN, H. B. (1972) "Toward a general theory of psychosocial deviance: the case of aggressive behavior." Social Science and Medicine 6 (5): 593-617.

KEMPE, C. H. et al. (1962) "The battered child syndrome." Journal of the American Medical Association 181 (July 7): 17-24.

KINSEY, A. C., W. B. POMEROY, and C. E. MARTIN (1948) Sexual Behavior in the Human Male. Philadelphia: W. B. Saunders Co.

KISER, D. J. (1944) Corpus Juris Secundum: A Complete Restatement of the Entire American Law as Developed by All Reported Cases. Brooklyn, N.Y.: American Law Book Co.

KLAUSNER, S. Z. [ed.] (1968) Why Man Takes Chances: Studies in Stress-Seeking. Garden City, N.Y.: Anchor Books.

KOMAROVSKY, M. (1940) The Unemployed Man and his Family. New York: Dryden Press. Pp. 449-457 in Paul F. Lazarsfeld and Morris Rosenberg [eds.] The Language of Social Research (1955). New York: Free Press.

——— (1967) Blue Collar Marriage. New York: Vintage Books.

LAING, R. D. (1969) The Politics of the Family and Other Essays. New York: Vintage Books.

LAING, R. D. and A. ESTERSON (1964) Sanity, Madness and the Family: Families of Schizophrenics. New York: Basic Books.

LARSEN, O. N. [ed.] (1968) Violence and the Mass Media. New York: Harper & Row.

LeMASTERS, E. E. (1957) "Parenthood as crisis." Marriage and Family Living 19 (November): 352-355.

LEON, C. A. (1969) "Unusual patterns of crime during 'la Violencia' in Colombia." American Journal of Psychiatry 125 (11): 1564-1575.

LEVINGER, G. (1966) "Sources of marital dissatisfaction among applicants for divorce." American Journal of Orthopsychiatry 26 (October): 803-807. Pp. 126-132 as reprinted in Paul H. Glasser and Louis N. Glasser [eds.] Families in Crisis. New York: Harper & Row.

LIEBOWITZ, J. (1972) "Child abuse: it's not the youngsters, but the parents who need rehabilitation." Sunday Herald Traveler and Boston Sunday Advertiser (November 26): 5, 10.

LIGHT, R. J. (1974) "Abused and neglected children in America: a study of alternative policies." Harvard Educational Review 43 (November): 556-598.

LINDZEY, G., H. D. WINSTON, and M. MANOSEVITZ (1963) "Early experience genotype and temperament in *mus musculus.*" Journal of Comparative Physiological Psychology 56 (3): 622-629.

LYMAN, S. M. and M. B. SCOTT (1970) A Sociology of the Absurd. New York: Appleton-Century-Crofts.

MacANDREW, C. and R. B. EDGERTON (1969) Drunken Comportment: A Social Explanation. Chicago: Aldine.

MATZA, D. (1964) Delinquency and Drift. New York: John Wiley.

McCAGHY, C. H. (1968) "Drinking and deviance disavowal: the case of child molesters." Social Problems 16 (1): 43-49.

MEAD, M. and F. C. MacGREGOR (1951) Growth and Culture: A Photographic Study of Balinese Children. New York: G. P. Putnam's Sons.

MERTON, R. K. (1938) "Social structure and anomie." American Sociological Review 3 (October): 672-682.

MILLER, N. E. (1941) "The frustration-aggression hypothesis." Psychological Review 48 (4): 337-342.

MILLER, W. B. (1958) "Lower class culture as a generating milieu of gang delinquency." Journal of Social Issues 14 (Summer): 5-19.

MONAHAN, T. P. and W. M. KEPHART (1954) "Divorce and desertion by religious and mixed religious groups." American Journal of Sociology 59 (March): 454-465.

Newsweek (1972) "Help for child abusers" (July 24): 66-69.

––– (1973a) "The deadliest city" (January 1): 20-21.

––– (1973b) "Britain: battered wives" (July 9): 39.

O'BRIEN, J. E. (1971) "Violence in divorce prone families." Journal of Marriage and the Family 33 (November): 692-698.

OWENS, D. J. and M. A. STRAUS (1973) "Childhood violence and adult approval of violence." Paper presented to the 1973 meetings of the American Orthopsychiatric Association.

PALMER, S. (1955) Understanding Other People. Greenwich, Conn.: Fawcett Publications.

––– (1962) The Psychology of Murder. New York: Thomas Y. Crowell Co.

––– (1972) The Violent Society. New Haven: College and University Press.

––– (1973) "High social integration as a source of deviance." British Journal of Sociology 24 (March): 93-100.

Parade (1971) "The wife beaters" (September 12): 13.

––– (1972) "Therapy for child abuse" (April 4): 10.

PARNAS, R. I. (1967) "The police response to domestic disturbance." Wisconsin Law Review 914 (Fall): 914-960.

PITTMAN, D. J. and W. HANDY (1964) "Patterns in criminal aggravated assault." Journal of Criminal Law, Criminology and Police Science 55 (4): 462-470.

POKORNY, A. D. (1965) "Human violence: a comparison of homicide, aggravated assault, suicide, and attempted suicide." Journal of Criminal Law, Criminology and Police Science 56 (December): 488-497.

POLSKY, N. (1969) Hustlers, Beats, and Others. Garden City, N.Y.: Anchor Books.

PRICE, W. H. and P. B. WHATMORE (1967) "Behavior disorders and patterns of crime among XYY males identified at a maximum security hospital." British Medical Journal 69 (1): 533-536.

RAINWATER, L., R. D. COLEMAN, and G. HANDEL (1959) Workingman's Wife. New York: Oceana Publications.

RANSFORD, H. E. (1968) "Isolation, powerlessness, and violence: a study of attitudes and participation in the Watts Riot." American Journal of Sociology 73 (March): 581-591.

RESNICK, P. J. (1969) "Child murder by parents: a psychiatric review of filicide." American Journal of Psychiatry 126 (3): 325-334.

ROBINSON, J. P., R. ATHANASIOU, and K. HEAD (1969) Measures of Occupational Attitudes and Occupational Characteristics. Ann Arbor, Mich.: Survey Research Center.

RUSK, H. A. and J. NOVEY (1955) "The impact of chronic illness on families." Marriage and Family Living 19 (May): 193-197.

SCHAFER, S. (1968) The Victim and His Criminal: A Study in Functional Responsibility. New York: Random House.

SCHATZMAN, L. and A. STRAUSS (1955) "Social class and modes of communication." American Journal of Sociology 60 (January): 329-338.

SCHONELL, F. J. and B. H. WATTS (1956) "A first survey of the effects of a subnormal child on the family unit." American Journal of Mental Deficiency 61 (July): 210-219.

SCHULTZ, L. G. (1960) "The wife assaulter." Journal of Social Therapy 6 (2): 103-111.

SEARS, R. R., E. MACCOBY, and H. LEVIN (1957) Patterns of Child Rearing. Evanston, Ill.: Row Peterson.

SHAH, S. (1970) "Report on the XYY chromosonal abnormality." National Institute of Mental Health conference report. Washington, D.C.: U.S. Government Printing Office.

SINGER, J. (1971) The Control of Aggression and Violence. New York: Academic Press.

SNELL, J. E., R. J. ROSENWALD, and A. ROBEY (1964) "The wifebeater's wife: a study of family interraction." Archives of General Psychiatry 11 (August): 107-113.

SPINETTA, J. J. and D. RIGLER (1972) "The child-abusing parent: a psychological review." Psychological Bulletin 77 (April): 296-304.

SPREY, J. (1969) "The family as a system in conflict." Journal of Marriage and the Family 31 (November): 699-706.

STARK, R. and J. McEVOY, III (1970) "Middle class violence." Psychology Today 4 (November): 52-65.

STEELE, B. F. and C. B. POLLOCK (1968) "A psychiatric study of parents who abuse infants and small children." Pp. 103-147 in Ray E. Helfer and C. Henry Kempe [eds.] The Battered Child. Chicago: University of Chicago Press.

STEINMETZ, S. K. and M. A. STRAUS (1973) "The Family as Cradle of Violence." Society 10 (6): 50-56.

——— (1974) Violence in the Family. New York: Dodd, Mead.

STOENNER, H. (1972) "Myths, stereotypes cloud public picture of abuse." Denver Post (August 8): 53-55.

STRAUS, M. A. (1973) "A general systems theory approach to the development of a theory of violence between family members." Social Science Information 12 (June): 105-125.

———, R. J. GELLES, and S. K. STEINMETZ (1973) "Theories, methods, and controversies in the study of violence between family members." Paper presented at the 1973 meetings of the American Sociological Association.

SWEET, W. H., F. ERVIN, and V. H. MARK (1969) "The relationship of violent behavior to focal cerebral disease." In S. Garattini and E. Siss [eds.] Aggressive Behavior. New York: John Wiley.

SYKES, G. M. and D. MATZA (1957) "Techniques of neutralization: a theory of delinquency." American Sociological Review 22 (December): 664-470.

TANAY, E. (1969) "Psychiatric study of homicide." American Journal of Psychiatry 125 (9): 1252-1258.

TRUNINGER, E. (1971) "Marital violence: the legal solutions." Hastings Law Journal 23 (November): 259-276.

U.S. Bureau of Census (1971a) General Population Characteristics: New Hampshire 1970. Washington, D.C.: U.S. Department of Commerce.

——— (1971b) Statistical Abstract of the United States (92d ed.). Washington, D.C.: U.S. Department of Commerce.

——— (1972) Census of Population: General Social and Economic

Characteristics, New Hampshire. Washington, D.C.: U.S. Department of Commerce.

U.S. Department of Health, Education and Welfare (1969) Bibliography on the Battered Child. Social and Rehabilitation Service, July.

VIDICH, A. J. and J. BENSMAN (1968) Small Town in Mass Society: Class, Power, and Religion in a Rural Community. Princeton, N.J.: Princeton University Press.

WASSERMAN, S. (1967) "The abused parent of the abused child." Children 14 (September/October): 175-179.

WERTHAM, F. (1949) The Show of Violence. Garden City, N.Y.: Doubleday.

WEST, D. J. (1966) Homicide Followed by Suicide. Cambridge, Mass.: Harvard University Press.

WHITEHURST, R. M. (1971) "Violence potential in extramarital sexual responses." Journal of Marriage and the Family 33 (November): 683-691.

——— (1974) "Violently jealous husbands." In Suzanne K. Steinmetz and Murray A. Straus [eds.] Violence and the Family. New York: Dodd, Mead.

WOLFGANG, M. E. (1957) "Victim-precipitated criminal homicide." Journal of Criminal Law, Criminology and Police Science 48 (June): 1-11.

——— (1958) Patterns in Criminal Homicide. New York: John Wiley.

——— and F. FERRACUTI (1967) The Subculture of Violence. London: Tavistock Publications.

YOUNG, L. R. (1964) Wednesday's Children: A Study of Child Neglect and Abuse. New York: McGraw-Hill.

ZALBA, S. R. (1971) "Battered children." Transaction 8 (July/August): 58-61.

# APPENDICES

# APPENDIX A

## THE RESPONDENTS AND THEIR FAMILIES

This section presents a demographic profile of the total sample of respondents and their families. In addition, it discusses the differences among the four groups (agency, agency neighbors, police, and police neighbors) for each of the factors discussed.

### Marital Status, Length of Marriage

Of the 80 respondents interviewed, 62 (78%) were married at the time, 11 (14%) were divorced, four (5%) were separated, and three (4%) were widowed (see Table 26). All of the 14 husbands interviewed were presently married. The majority of the broken marriages (divorced, separated, widowed) were among the agency families and the police sample. The least marital disruption was found in the sample of neighbors of agency and police families. In addition, 13 of the respondents had been previously married.

### TABLE 26
### MARITAL STATUS OF RESPONDENTS BY
### SOURCE OF RESPONDENT
### (By Percent)

|  | Marital Status | | | |
|---|---|---|---|---|
|  | Married | Divorced | Separated | Widowed |
| Agency Families (N=20) | 75 | 20 | 5 | 0 |
| Agency Neighbors (N=20) | 90 | 10 | 0 | 0 |
| Police Families (N=20) | 65 | 10 | 15 | 10 |
| Police Neighbors (N=20) | 80 | 15 | 0 | 5 |
| Total (N=80) | 78 | 14 | 5 | 4 |

The mean length of the marriages of those respondents who were married was 11.4 years (Table 27). The agency respondents generally were married longer (13.6 years) than their neighbors (12.8 years), the police families (8.7 years), or the police neighbors (10.0 years). This may indicate that families that seek agency help do so after a number of years of marriage. The fact that the length of marriage of the police sample was less than the other groups leads to the hypothesis that individuals who call the police to intervene do so in the earlier stages of their marriage. It may be that problems that result in police intervention in the first years of marriage either get solved in the later years, lead to divorce, or, as Truninger (1971) suggests, the family finds that the police and the legal system are not much help in dealing with family strife, and thus, they do not call the police again after the first couple of episodes.

### TABLE 27
### LENGTH OF RESPONDENT'S MARRIAGE BY
### SOURCE OF RESPONDENT*
#### (By Percent)

|  | Length of Marriage | | | | | |
|---|---|---|---|---|---|---|
|  | 1 week to 5 yrs | 6 to 10 yrs | 11-15 yrs | 16-20 yrs | 21+ yrs | Mean Length |
| Agency Families (N=15) | 13 | 33 | 20 | 7 | 27 | 13.6 |
| Agency Neighbors (N=18) | 33 | 22 | 11 | 6 | 28 | 12.8 |
| Police Families (N=13) | 62 | 0 | 8 | 15 | 15 | 8.7 |
| Police Neighbors (N=16) | 44 | 19 | 12 | 12 | 12 | 10.0 |
| Total (N=62) | 37 | 19 | 13 | 10 | 21 | 11.4 |

*does not include respondents who were divorced, separated, or widowed

## Number of Children

The average number of children in the respondents' families was three (Table 28). The agency families had the most children (average of 4.0) and the agency neighbors and police neighbors had the least (average of 2.9). The police families had an average of 3.2 children. The

## TABLE 28
## NUMBER OF CHILDREN BY SOURCE OF RESPONDENT
### (By Percent)

| | Number of Children | | | | | | | | |
| | 0 | 1 | 2 | 3 | 4 | 5 | 6 | 7+ | Mean |
|---|---|---|---|---|---|---|---|---|---|
| Agency Families (N=20) | 0 | 5 | 35 | 20 | 30 | 5 | 0 | 5 | 4.0 |
| Agency Neighbors (N=20) | 5 | 20 | 10 | 40 | 10 | 10 | 0 | 5 | 2.9 |
| Police Families (N=20) | 0 | 15 | 30 | 10 | 20 | 15 | 10 | 0 | 3.2 |
| Police Neighbors (N=20) | 5 | 10 | 40 | 20 | 5 | 5 | 10 | 5 | 2.9 |
| Total (N=80) | 3 | 13 | 29 | 23 | 16 | 9 | 5 | 4 | 3.0 |

fact that the agency families had the highest average number of children may be a function of this group's longer average length of marriage. In addition, families with more children also may be more prone to turn to a social work agency for help in husband-wife or parent-child problems.

### Education, Occupation, Income

In examining educational attainment, data were gathered on education of both the respondent and the spouse. Thirty-five of the husbands (44%) had not completed high school, 24 (30%) had graduated high school, 16 (20%) had some college, while the remaining five (6%) had completed college or had gone on for post-graduate work (Table 29). Agency-neighbor husbands had the most education. None had less than some high school, while seven (35%) had at least some college. The police husbands had less education than husbands in neighbor families. Surprisingly, the agency husbands had the lowest educational attainment: 13 (65%) had not completed high school. (It was thought that families who sought agency help would have more education than their neighbors or families who called the police to intervene in family strife, but not a single husband in the agency families completed college.)

Interestingly, the wives had slightly more education than the husbands. Only 24 of the wives (30%) did not complete high school, and 41 (51%) had graduated high school. When it comes to college education, the wives fared less well, with only 10 (13%) having some college and the same five as the husbands (6%) graduating college (Table 29).

TABLE 29

## EDUCATION BY SEX AND SOURCE OF RESPONDENT
### (By Percent)

| | Education | | | | |
|---|---|---|---|---|---|
| | Grammer School less than 9th grade | Some High School | High School Graduate | Some College | College Graduate or Higher |
| **Agency Families:** | | | | | |
| Husbands (N=20) | 35 | 30 | 20 | 15 | 0 |
| Wives (N=20) | 25 | 10 | 50 | 10 | 5 |
| **Agency Neighbors:** | | | | | |
| Husbands (N=20) | 0 | 30 | 35 | 20 | 15 |
| Wives (N=20) | 5 | 35 | 35 | 15 | 10 |
| **Police Families:** | | | | | |
| Husbands (N=20) | 10 | 40 | 30 | 15 | 5 |
| Wives (N=20) | 20 | 10 | 60 | 10 | 0 |
| **Police Neighbors:** | | | | | |
| Husbands (N=20) | 5 | 25 | 35 | 30 | 5 |
| Wives (N=20) | 5 | 10 | 60 | 15 | 10 |
| **Total:** | | | | | |
| Husbands (N=80) | 13 | 31 | 30 | 20 | 6 |
| Wives (N=80) | 14 | 16 | 51 | 13 | 6 |

The education of the wives did not reflect patterns similar to the husbands. Wives of the police neighbors were better educated than the other wives: 17 of these women (85%) had either graduated high school or gone beyond high school. Wives in police families were slightly less educated than their comparative numbers next door: 12 (70%) had at least graduated high school. Wives of agency neighbors were better educated than the wives who went to agencies—only one had less than some high school, and five (25%) went on to college.

The agency wives were the least educated wives of the four groups: five (25%) had less than a high school education and only three (15%) went beyond high school.

The occupations of the husbands ranged from unemployed to professional-managers (Table 30). The professional-managers consisted mostly of engineers. No doctors, lawyers, or dentists were in the population interviewed. Most of the husbands were either operatives (machine operators, cooks, bartenders, and so on) or laborers (construction work, truck drivers, and so on).

**TABLE 30**
## OCCUPATION OF HUSBANDS

| Occupation | Percent  (N=80) |
| --- | :---: |
| Professional Technical Workers | 8 |
| Managers, Proprietors | 6 |
| Sales and Clerical Workers | 6 |
| Craftsmen, Foremen | 16 |
| Military Personnel (Enlisted) | 9 |
| Operatives, Cooks, Bartenders | 22 |
| Laborers, Truck Drivers | 20 |
| Unemployed | 13 |

In order to get a sense of how the husbands' occupations compared to each other, the Bureau of Census occupational status score was used (as given in Robinson, Athanasiou, Head, 1969: 357). These scores are based on 1960 percentile data on income and education for the general population:

The percentile norms on which these scores are based are interpreted as follows: Only two percent of the population had more than four years of college training and only six percent of the population reported a family income of over $10,000 in 1960. Thus, a person having both characteristics would score 98 on education and 94 on income. His average score of 96 would be added in with those of other people in his occupation to determine the overall status score for that occupation.

The agency husbands had the lowest means status score while their neighbors had the highest. Police families and neighbors had similar status scores, with the neighbors slightly higher (Table 31).

In examining the occupation of the wives, more than half of the wives (58%) did not have jobs or were housewives (Table 32). Many of the women who did work, worked as secretaries, waitresses, or domestic help. (See Table 31 for data on occupational status scores of wives.)

An artifact of the sampling technique contributed to the most significant difference between the wives in terms of occupation. While 16 agency-neighbor wives (80%), 14 police family wives (70%), and 10 police-neighbor wives (50%) did not work, only 6 agency wives (30%) did not work. This came about because only the agency families were called in advance and had made appointments to be interviewed. Thus, when working agency wives consented to be interviewed, they sched-

**TABLE 31**
## OCCUPATIONAL STATUS BY SEX AND
## SOURCE OF RESPONDENT*
### (By Percent)

| | Occupational Status (Bureau of Census) | | | | | |
|---|---|---|---|---|---|---|
| | No Job or House-wife (0) | Low** (1-39) | Medium** (40-60) | High** (61-80) | Profes-sional Manager-ial (81-99) | Mean*** Status Score |
| **Agency Families:** | | | | | | |
| Husbands (N=20) | 20 | 30 | 20 | 25 | 5 | 37.6 |
| Wives (N=20) | 30 | 30 | 5 | 10 | 25 | 58.4 |
| **Agency Neighbors:** | | | | | | |
| Husbands (N=20) | 10 | 10 | 25 | 30 | 25 | 58.4 |
| Wives (N=20) | 80 | 5 | 0 | 0 | 15 | 76.0 |
| **Police Families:** | | | | | | |
| Husbands (N=20) | 5 | 40 | 20 | 25 | 10 | 44.8 |
| Wives (N=20) | 70 | 15 | 5 | 5 | 5 | 49.8 |
| **Police Neighbors:** | | | | | | |
| Husbands (N=20) | 15 | 25 | 15 | 25 | 20 | 47.9 |
| Wives (N=20) | 50 | 25 | 0 | 20 | 5 | 52.7 |
| **Total:** | | | | | | |
| Husbands (N=80) | 13 | 26 | 20 | 26 | 15 | 47.2 |
| Wives (N=80) | 58 | 19 | 3 | 9 | 13 | 57.3 |

*occupational status score for husbands of widows based on their occupation when they died
**categories formed by natural breaks in data
***for husbands the mean score includes husbands with no jobs. For wives mean score only includes wives who work (excludes no jobs and housewives)

**TABLE 32**
## OCCUPATION OF WIVES

| Occupation | Percent (N=80) |
|---|---|
| Managers, Proprietors | 5 |
| Nurses | 4 |
| Teachers | 4 |
| Secretaries, Clerical Workers | 10 |
| Waitresses, Hostesses, Domestic Help | 15 |
| Laborers | 5 |
| Unemployed/Housewives | 58 |

### TABLE 33
### TOTAL FAMILY INCOME BY SOURCE OF RESPONDENT
(By Percent)

| | Total Family Income | | | | | | |
|---|---|---|---|---|---|---|---|
| | under $3,000 | $3,000-$4,999 | $5,000-$6,999 | $7,000-$9,999 | $10,000-$14,999 | $15,000-$19,999 | $20,000 or higher |
| Agency Families (N=20) | 0 | 15 | 15 | 30 | 30 | 10 | 0 |
| Agency Neighbors (N=20) | 10 | 10 | 10 | 20 | 30 | 10 | 10 |
| Police Families (N=20) | 15 | 20 | 15 | 20 | 30 | 0 | 0 |
| Police Neighbors (N=20) | 0 | 20 | 25 | 15 | 30 | 10 | 0 |
| Total (N=80) | 6 | 16 | 16 | 21 | 30 | 8 | 3 |

uled the day and time for a time they did not work. In all the other cases, the person at home was interviewed, and that was likely to be a wife who did not work.

The range of total family income in the respondents' families was from under $3,000 to as high as $25,000 per year. The agency-neighbor families had the highest income—10 (50%) made more than $10,000 in 1971. Police families were the lowest in terms of family income—no family made more than $14,999 and seven families (35%) made less than $5,000 (Table 33).

## Religion

Looking at the husbands, 37 (46%) were Catholic, 35 (44%) Protestant, one (1%) Jewish, and seven (9%) had no religious preference (Table 34). Forty-two of the wives (53%) were Catholic, 32 (40%) Protestant, one (1%) Jewish, and five (6%) had no religious preference (Table 34). The bulk of the Catholic families came from the agency and agency-neighbor sample, which was from the highly Catholic community of Manchester, New Hampshire. The proportion of Catholics was much lower for the police and police-neighbor families, who lived in Portsmouth.

### TABLE 34
### RELIGION BY SEX AND SOURCE OF RESPONDENT
### (By Percent)

| | Religion | | | |
|---|---|---|---|---|
| | Catholic | Protestant | Jewish | None |
| **Agency Families:** | | | | |
| Husbands (N=20) | 45 | 40 | 5 | 10 |
| Wives (N=20) | 55 | 40 | 5 | 0 |
| **Agency Neighbors:** | | | | |
| Husbands (N=20) | 75 | 25 | 0 | 0 |
| Wives (N=20) | 75 | 25 | 0 | 0 |
| **Police Families:** | | | | |
| Husbands (N=20) | 25 | 55 | 0 | 20 |
| Wives (N=20) | 40 | 40 | 0 | 20 |
| **Police Neighbors:** | | | | |
| Husbands (N=20) | 40 | 55 | 0 | 5 |
| Wives (N=20) | 40 | 55 | 0 | 5 |
| **Total:** | | | | |
| Husbands (N=80) | 46 | 44 | 1 | 9 |
| Wives (N=80) | 53 | 40 | 1 | 6 |

## Age

Most of the respondents and their spouses were young. Thirty of the husbands (39%) and 34 of the wives (43%) were under 30 years of age. The mean age of the husbands was 37.4, while the mean age of the wives was 34.7 (Table 35). The mean ages of the husbands and wives for the agency, agency neighbors, police, and police neighbors were fairly similar. The exception was that the husbands and wives of the police neighbors were decidedly younger. No explanation for this difference can be provided as a result of the sampling technique.

### TABLE 35
### AGE BY SEX AND SOURCE OF RESPONDENT
#### (By Percent)

|  | Age | | | | |
|---|---|---|---|---|---|
|  | 19-30 | 31-40 | 41-50 | 51 or older | Mean |
| **Agency Families:** | | | | | |
| Husbands (N=20) | 25 | 25 | 40 | 10 | 38.2 |
| Wives      (N=20) | 30 | 40 | 25 | 5 | 35.5 |
| **Agency Neighbors:** | | | | | |
| Husbands (N=20) | 45 | 20 | 10 | 25 | 38.7 |
| Wives      (N=20) | 55 | 10 | 10 | 25 | 36.6 |
| **Police Families:** | | | | | |
| Husbands (N=18)* | 39 | 11 | 28 | 22 | 41.2 |
| Wives      (N=20) | 35 | 30 | 30 | 5 | 35.2 |
| **Police Neighbors:** | | | | | |
| Husbands (N=19)* | 47 | 32 | 21 | 0 | 33.1 |
| Wives      (N=20) | 50 | 30 | 20 | 0 | 31.6 |
| **Total:** | | | | | |
| Husbands (N=77)* | 39 | 22 | 25 | 14 | 37.4 |
| Wives      (N=80) | 43 | 28 | 21 | 9 | 34.7 |

*excludes husbands who were deceased at time of interview

## Race

As New Hampshire has a small non-white population (6%) to begin with (U.S. Bureau of Census, 1971a), it was unlikely that many non-whites would be interviewed. One police family and one police neighbor were black, while one white respondent who had called the police was married to a black husband.

*Summary*. In the sampling design it was expected that the agency families would be predominantly middle-class families while the police families more likely would be from the lower-socioeconomic ranges. It also was feared that the entire sample might not reflect a total range of education, occupation, and income. In the sample actually studied, the agency families *do not* reflect the "middle-class bias" in either their education or occupation. The agency families turned out to be similar to, if not lower than police families for all factors except income. Second, although no "elites" (such as doctors, lawyers, dentists, or professors, or families with very high incomes) were interviewed, there is a range of education, occupation, and income in both the overall sample and for each of the 20 families in the four groups.

One important factor in comparing the samples is that the agency families are significantly lower than their *neighbors* in terms of education, occupational status of both spouses, and total family income. This lack of "resources" may be one reason why they, as opposed to their neighbors, sought out agency help for family problems. While police neighbors are somewhat more educated and have more income and better jobs than families where the police have been called in, these differences are not as large as for agency families.

Looking at the other aspects of the families, the sample consists mostly of young families. Most of the spouses are under 30 and the mean length of the marriages is 11 years. The mean number of children (3) may be increased in this sample over time, because the respondents are still in their childbearing years (in fact, a number of the wives interviewed were pregnant).

The religious and racial makeup of the sample reflects the religious and racial characterists of Manchester and Portsmouth. (See Appendix B for a brief description of Portsmouth and Manchester.) There were few non-whites and a large number of Catholics, particularly from the Manchester area.

*Strength and Limitations of the Sampling Method and Sample.* There are a number of limitations with the sampling method and the final sample interviewed. First, because the police and agency samples had to be drawn from different cities, any attempt to compare the agency families and their neighbors with the police families and their neighbors is confounded by the characteristics of the individual cities such as different unemployment rates (Manchester is lower) and the difference in religious and racial characteristics of the two cities. Second, because no appointments were made with the 60 nonagency families, the nonagency families had a low number of working wives.

Third, although great efforts were made to include husbands, the resulting sample of predominantly female respondents will provide mainly the wife's perspective on intrafamily violence. Last, the technique of selecting families from private social work agencies, police records, and these families' neighbors apparently systematically excluded upper-middle-class and upper-class families from the sample. Although a range of families is included in the sample, there still were no families who made more than $25,000 a year, nor were there any respondents who were doctors, lawyers, dentists, or professors.

Despite these limitations, there were a number of strengths in this sampling method. One strength is that a range (even though somewhat limited) of families was included. The sample did not reflect any overall working-class, lower-class, or middle-class bias. In terms of socio-economic status, the sample ranged from lower (low income, occupational status, grade school education) to middle class (incomes as high as $25,000, "some college" or college graduates, and managerial or professional occupations). In addition, there were families with only one child and families with as many as nine.

A second strength of the sampling method was the sampling of a comparison group, a group of families that could be used in comparing violent families to nonviolent families. By sampling neighbors, the sample included a number of families with no violent incidents. Perhaps the greatest strength of the sampling method is that it provided families where violence had occurred. The entire research hinged on whether this technique of sampling would provide a number of families where there had been violent occurrences between husbands and wives—the focused sample allowed us to contact and interview those families.

# APPENDIX B

## MANCHESTER AND PORTSMOUTH

### Manchester

The city of Manchester is centrally located in the southern part of New Hampshire. Manchester is the state's largest city with a population of 95,309. The population has a mixed ethnic background, with the largest single ethnic group being of French-Canadian origin. French is the mother tongue of almost 40% of the native population. Manchester has a non-white population of 5%. The median school years completed for Manchester residents is 11.6. Manchester is the financial and economic center of the state. Its location along the Merrimack River led to the development of major textile and shoe industries. Of late, these industries are on the decline and the city's economic base is shifting towards other industries such as electronics and plastics. As of 1970, 3.5% of the male-over-16 civilian labor force was unemployed (U.S. Bureau of Census, 1972).

### Portsmouth

Located in the southeast portion of the state on the Atlantic Ocean, Portsmouth is New Hampshire's port city. Portsmouth's 26,059 residents come from a variety of ethnic backgrounds, but unlike Manchester, there is no significant group with a non-English mother tongue. Portsmouth has a 5.1% non-white population. The median school years completed by city residents is 12.4. With Pease Air Force Base and a Navy shipyard in the city, the economy of Portsmouth is somewhat dependent on the continuing operation of these facilities. The unemployment rate for men over 16 was 4.1 in 1970 (U.S. Bureau of Census, 1972).

## LETTER INTRODUCING PROJECT TO
## SOCIAL WORK STAFF

Date: May 25, 1972
To: Social Work Staff
From: Alice White

As you know from Mr. Chicoine's remarks at the annual meeting, the agency is participating with the Sociology Department at the University of New Hampshire on a "program designed to train sociologists specializing in research on the family, in the context of community agencies."

The first project in which Child and Family Services of New Hampshire will be involved is a study by Richard Gelles, a doctoral candidate, on "Family Problems and the Use of Physical Force in Problem Solving." Mr. Gelles says in a preliminary introduction to the subject that "The ideal picture of the American family is one of a stable unit bound together by harmony, love, and gentleness. But the family also exists as a system which is characterized by stress, strain, and conflict. One of the important, but little understood aspects of this "conflict" view of the family is the use of physical force by family members in their day to day life together. While some researchers have examined the more extreme forms of violence in families, such as child battering, homicide, very little attention has been focused on the day to day, patterned use of force.... Since knowledge about the meaning and use of physical force within the family may shed light on some of the problems the families face and the way they go about solving these problems, we have proposed an in-depth study of force in the family."

Mr. Gelles' method of data gathering is to be the "unstructured, conversational interview." He believes that this will "afford the opportunity to reach the study's goals of obtaining rich, detailed and in-depth information about the familial use of physical force without disturbing the subjects by making direct questions about sensitive areas."

Mr. Gelles is asking our help in securing "subject families."

Would you please review your open case load and your closings so far in 1972 and list, on the attached sheet of paper, the name and address of families who may have reported to you forceful incidents or where you have observed or been told about serious family conflict, marital disagreements, or parent-child problems.

After the name and town of residence please indicate why you have included this family. For example: "the wife reported . . ." or, "relatives reported . . ." or, "this was a hunch of mine . . ." and the family's stated reason for coming to the agency.

All the families that you list may not be interviewed, and of course, the agency will protect the rights of clients, guarantee the confidentiality, and obtain their permission to be interviewed. This request is for a tentative list in order to get some idea of how large a sample we might be able to provide Mr. Gelles.

Please return to me by June 9, 1972.

# UNIVERSITY OF NEW HAMPSHIRE
## DURHAM, NEW HAMPSHIRE 03824

COLLEGE OF LIBERAL ARTS
Department of Sociology and Anthropology
Social Science Center

To Whom It May Concern:

This is to certify that Richard Gelles is an interviewer employed by the Family Problem Solving Study being carried out at the University of New Hampshire. He can identify himself by presenting a University of New Hampshire identification card.

This is also to guarantee that all information will be kept in the strictest confidence.

It you have any questions about this, please feel free to phone me at my office (862-1800) or home (659-3832).

Thank you for your cooperation.

Sincerely,

Murray A. Straus
Professor

# INDEXES

# AUTHOR INDEX

Adelson, L., 26
Athanasiou, R., 209

Bach, G., 162
Bakan, D., 153, 171
Bales, R., 88
Bandura, A., 172, 178
Bennie, E., 150
Bensman, J., 29
Blumberg, M., 59
Boll, E., 97
Bossard, J., 97
Boston Globe, 20, 21, 140

Cavan, R., 153
Cohen, A., 27
Coleman, R., 29
Corning, C., 48
Corning, P., 48
Coser, L., 90, 120, 152, 172, 182, 188
Cuber, J., 29

Davis, F., 94, 114
Dow, T., 153
Dyer, E., 146, 153

Edgerton, R., 94, 114, 116
Eron, L., 20
Esterson, A., 25
Etzioni, A., 25, 152, 172, 188

Farberow, N., 28
Faulkner, R., 87
Ferracuti, F., 90, 114, 120, 172

Gelles, R., 36, 85, 90, 171, 172, 188, 190
Gerth, H., 117
Gil, D., 22, 23, 26, 55, 149, 156, 171, 190
Gillen, J., 77, 111, 165, 171
Glaser, B., 188
Goffman, E., 96
Gold, M., 171, 172, 188
Goode, W., 120, 127, 136, 137, 142, 152, 157, 164, 165, 171
Gribbon, A., 114
Guttmacher, M., 77, 111, 113, 170, 172

Hall, O., 29
Handel, G., 29, 88
Handy, W., 22, 53, 95, 105, 111, 190
Harroff, P., 29
Head, K., 209
Helfer, R., 22
Hentig, H. von, 155, 156
Hess, R., 88
Hill, R., 153
Hobbs, D., 146, 153
Humphreys, L., 29

Jackson, J., 153

Kaplan, H., 81, 166, 172, 188
Kempe, C., 22, 28, 88, 171
Kephart, W., 127
Kinsey, A., 31
Kiser, D., 116
Komarovsky, M., 29, 39, 73, 74, 86, 123

Laing, R., 25
Larsen, O., 169
Lefkowitz, M., 20
LeMasters, E., 146, 153
Leon, C., 171
Levin, H., 20
Levinger, G., 23, 50, 192
Liebowitz, J., 23
Light, R., 23
Lyman, S., 48, 57, 86

MacAndrew, C., 94, 114, 116
Maccoby, E., 20
Martin, C., 31
Matza, D., 68, 117
McCaghy, C., 94, 114, 115
McEvoy, J., 27, 58, 59, 61
Merton, R., 185
Miller, W., 27
Mills, C., 117
Monahan, T., 127

Newsweek, 21, 23, 192
Novey, J., 153

O'Brien, J., 20, 23, 136, 137, 142, 192
Owens, D., 85, 172, 179, 188

Palmer, S., 21, 144, 152, 156, 170
Parade, 22, 128
Parnas, R., 58
Pittman, D., 22, 53, 95, 105, 111, 190
Pokorny, A., 22, 95, 96, 100, 105, 190
Pollock, C., 55, 171
Pomeroy, W., 31

Rainwater, L., 29
Resnick, P., 55
Robey, A., 37, 111, 121, 143
Robinson, J., 209
Rosenwald, R., 37, 111, 121, 143

Ross, D., 172, 178
Ross, S., 172, 178
Rusk, H., 153

Schafer, S., 156
Schatzman, L., 29
Schonell, F., 153
Schultz, L., 143
Sclare, A., 150
Scott, M., 48, 57, 86
Sears, R., 20
Singer, J., 28, 172, 174
Snell, J., 37, 111, 121, 143
Sprey, J., 119
Stark, R., 27, 58, 59, 61
Steele, B., 55, 171
Steinmetz, S., 20, 85, 145, 183, 188, 190
Stoenner, H., 23
Straus, M., 20, 29, 70, 85, 145, 172, 179,
   183, 188, 190
Strauss, A., 188
Sykes, G., 68, 117

Tanay, E., 170
Tredgold, R., 128
Truninger, E., 21, 206

U.S. Bureau of Census, 213, 217
U.S. Department of Health, Education,
   and Welfare, 20

Vidich, A., 29

Walder, L., 20
Watts, B., 153
Whitehurst, R., 23, 82
Wolfgang, M., 21, 22, 26, 52, 77, 90, 95,
   96, 99, 100, 103, 105, 111, 114, 118,
   120, 156, 160, 163, 172
Wyden, P., 162

Zalba, S., 55

# SUBJECT INDEX

Accounts of intrafamily violence, 48, 57-58, 86, 115, 170, 175, 176, 180-181
Achieved status vs. ascribed status, 137
Actors' perception of violence, 89-90
Age
    and punishment of children, 91 fn.
    and conjugal violence, 109, 121-122
    difference between husband and wife and conjugal violence, 137
    of respondents, 213, 214
Agency cases, selection of, 33-34, 215
Aggravated assault (*see* assault)
Alcohol and violence, 43, 77-80, 89, 94, 103, 105, 111-118, 161-162, 166-167,
    187
Alcoholism and the family, 153 fn.
"All in the Family," 175
"An eye for an eye," 66-67
Anniversary
    and violence, 106
Assault, 14, 19, 22, 23, 53, 88, 95, 104-105, 111, 169, 190
Atlanta, 21

Bathroom
    as location of conjugal violence, 96, 99
Battered-wife shelter, 14
Battered wives, 13, 14
Bedroom as location of conjugal violence, 95, 96, 98, 99, 103
Birthday and violence, 106
Bureau of Census, occupational status score, 209

Calculus of punishment, 68, 178
Cambodia, 78
Child abuse, 20, 22-23, 24, 26, 28, 34, 35, 47, 55, 88-89, 90, 149, 150, 156, 169,
    171, 190, 193
    "prenatal," 146

Child and Family Services, 33
Child beating (*see* child abuse)
Child molestation, 115
"Child proofing" the home, 65
Christmas, 30, 106-107
Chronic illness, 153 fn.
Colombia, study of violent bandits in, 171
Conduct of the interview, 39-43
Conflict model, 14, 119
Conjugal violence
    incidence of, 43, 47-53, 183-184, 191, 192
    methods of, 52-53
    (*see* also husband to wife and wife to husband)
Consensus model, 14, 119
Consensus theory, 13
Contacting subjects, 36-39
Cramden, Ralph, 158
Criminal homicide (*see* homicide)
Culture of violence, 120, 130, 172, 190 (*see* also subculture of violence)

Day of the week and conjugal violence, 94, 104-105
Definition of the situation, 86, 87, 88, 89
Delinquent gangs, violence in, 27
Detroit, 21
Deviance disavowal, 94, 113-117
Deviant behavior, 89, 115
"Dick Van Dyke Show, The," 175
Dining room as location of conjugal violence, 96
Disabled child, 153 fn.
Discipline of children and violence, 65-70
Divorce, 23, 44 fn., 50, 140-141, 193
    petitioners, 15, 50

Education
    differences between husband and wife and conjugal violence, 123, 137-139,
        145, 188
    husband's and conjugal violence, 122, 142
    level of and conjugal violence, 43, 109, 121, 122-123, 128, 129, 130, 132,
        137, 189, 192
    respondents' level, 207-208, 214, 215
    wife's and conjugal violence, 122-123, 130
England, 14
Ethnicity and punishment of children, 91 fn.
"Expressive" violence, 85-90
Extra-marital sexual relations, 82, 147

Family disturbance calls to police, 34-35
Family roles and conjugal violence, 136-143

Family size and conjugal violence, 43
Family structure and conjugal violence, 109, 120-121, 123, 136-152, 188
"Father Knows Best," 175
Father to child violence, 141
    incidence of, 55
FBI, 21
Filicide, 22
Frigidity and conjugal violence, 147
Frustration, 16, 74-75, 76, 102, 120, 123, 128, 130, 132, 142-143, 148, 152, 160, 170, 175, 185, 188
Frustration-aggression theory, 190
Functionalist theory, 13
Funneling technique, 30-32

"Generalized other," 131
Genetic theory of violence, 182 fn.
*Godfather, The,* 145
*Gone with the Wind,* 145

Hockey (*see* violence in professional hockey)
Home as "backstage," 96
"Honeymooners," 158
Holiday and conjugal violence (*see* also Christmas and New Year's), 106
Homicide, 14, 19, 20, 21, 22, 23, 24, 26, 28, 94-95, 96, 98, 99, 100, 103, 104-105, 111, 116, 156, 169, 170-172, 183, 190
Homosexuality, problems of research on, 29
Husband to wife violence, incidence of, 50-51

Impotence and conjugal violence, 148
Income and conjugal violence, 43, 121, 125-126, 130, 132, 189, 192
    of respondents, 212, 214, 215
Informal interview (*see* interview technique)
"Instrumental" violence, 85-90
Integration theory, 13
"Interaction Process Analysis," 88
Intermarriage, 150
Interview technique, 29-32, 39-40, 50, 94
Intrafamily violence, meanings of, 57-85
Isolation and conjugal violence, 16, 43, 76, 109, 110, 121, 132-136, 184, 187

Jealous husbands, 23, 82
Jealous wives, 84
*Journal of Marriage and the Family,* 20

Kitchen as location of conjugal violence, 95, 96, 97, 98, 102, 103, 110

Learning theory, 190
Legitimate vs. illegitimate violence, 58, 70, 84, 85-90

Length of marriage of respondents, 205-206, 214
Living room as location of conjugal violence, 95, 96, 98, 99

Manchester, New Hampshire, 33, 34, 40, 106, 214, 217
Marital dissolution, 119 (*see* also divorce)
Marital status of respondents, 205-206
Massachusetts, 23
Meanings of intrafamily violence, 48
Mentally ill, 183
Middle-class bias in sampling agency cases, 34
Middle-class families and physical abuse, 50, 214
Miscarriage, caused by violence, 146
Mother to child violence, incidence of, 55
Murder (*see* Homicide)

National Commission on the Causes and Prevention of Violence, 58, 179
Neighbors of case families, selection of, 35
Neutralization of violence, 68-70, 74, 114, 117, 118
New Year's, 30, 83, 106-107
New York, 23
"Normal" violence, 58-70, 75, 176
Norms
    *re* conjugal violence, 120, 136, 169
    *re* violence, 170, 189
Number of children, 206-207, 214
    and conjugal violence, 149-150

Objectives of the research, 43
Occupation of respondents, 208-212, 214
Occupational mobility, 143
Occupational status
    and conjugal violence, 43, 121, 124-125, 130, 132, 137, 189, 192
    differences between husband and wife and conjugal violence, 109, 125, 137-139, 145, 188
    husband's and conjugal violence, 124, 131, 142
    measurement of, 209-212
    of respondents, 208-212, 217
    wife's and conjugal violence, 125, 130
"One way" violence, 80-82

Parent-child violence, 20, 26, 34, 170, 190
    incidence of, 47, 53-57
    (*see* also father to child and mother to child)
Parental violence
    methods of, 56
Parenthood as family crisis, 146, 153 fn.
Philadelphia, 21, 105, 156
Physicians, and reporting of child abuse, 28
Police blotter cases, selection of, 34

Police intervention in family quarrels, 58
Political assassination, 14
Population and sample, 32-36, 90 fn., 191, 209
Portsmouth, New Hampshire, 34, 214, 217
Pregnancy and violence, 30, 145-147, 184, 189, 193
Presence or absence of other people and violence, 94, 107-110
Private vs. public violence, 93-94
"Protective-reaction" violence, 78-80
Psychological violence, 24, 25, 189
Psychopathological traits, 185
Punishment of children, 20, 27, 171, 175, 185

Race of respondents, 213, 214
Religion and conjugal violence, 43, 121, 127-128
    of respondents, 212, 214
Religious differences and conjugal violence, 110, 150-151, 189
Research on sensitive issues, 28-29
Resource theory of violence, 120, 130, 190
Role models for violence, 44, 170, 172, 178, 189
Role of the victim in acts of violence, 155-157 (*see* also victim-precipitated
    violence)
Role reversal, 143-145
Role stress, 124
Role structure, 16

Sampling technique (*see* population and sample)
Sarcasm, 167
Secondary conflict, 70, 113
Secondary violence, 70-73
Selective inattention, 13, 15
Self-attitude theory of violence, 172, 190
Self-esteem, 132, 165-167, 187
Sex and conjugal violence, 82-85, 89, 98-99, 103, 104, 113, 147-148, 160-161,
    166-167, 187
Sexual behavior, research on, 31
Sibling violence, 26
Size of family and conjugal violence (*see* number of children)
Social isolation and conjugal violence (*see* isolation and conjugal violence)
Socialization, 23, 82, 109, 170-172, 182, 185, 187, 189, 190
Social structure, 16, 43, 152, 182, 184
    family's location in and conjugal violence, 121-132, 152, 184, 190, 192
Social structure of violence, 90 fn.
Social structural theory of violence, 16, 120, 130, 172, 187-190
Socioeconomic status, and punishment of children, 91 fn
"Spare the rod and spoil the child," 62, 176
Spatial dynamics of conjugal violence, 96-99, 102
Spatial patterns of conjugal violence, 16, 43, 94-99
Status inconsistency, 137, 143
Stress, and conjugal violence, 74, 97, 105, 107, 110, 120, 123, 126, 128-130,
    132, 146, 148, 149-152, 155, 185, 187, 188-189, 190

Stressor events, 153 fn.
Structural stress and conjugal violence (*see* stress and conjugal violence)
Subcultural of violence, 90 fn., 120, 190
Suicide, 189
    threats of, 73

Tape recording the interviews, 39-40, 45 fn.
Techniques of neutralization (*see* neutralization of violence)
Television violence, effects on children, 169
Temporal dynamics of conjugal violence
    time of day, 100-104
    day of the week, 105
Temporal patterns of conjugal violence, 16, 43, 94, 99-107
Threats of violence, 73-74
Threshold of violence, 193
Time of day and conjugal violence, 94, 99-104, 110
Time of year and conjugal violence, 94, 105-107
"Time out" mechanism, 94, 114, 116-117
Typology of intrafamily violence, 43, 48, 85-90

Unemployment, 153 fn.
Unemployment and conjugal violence, 124, 128-129, 152, 189
University of New Hampshire, 44 fn.
United States government, 78
Unstructured interview, 29-32
Unwanted pregnancy, 43

Verbal attacks, 157-164
Victimology, 156
Victim-precipitated homicide, 156, 160
Victim-precipitated conjugal violence, 59, 75, 86-90, 158, 187
Vietnam, 14, 78
Violence, approved of, 44, 170, 171-172, 175, 179-180, 189
    as learned behavior, 181-182
    definition of, 24-25
    imitation of, 172, 178
    in professional hockey, 87
    observation of as a child, 172-173, 176, 179
    social meanings of, 15
    used to teach and control children, 63-65
Violence in the street vs. violence in the home, 93-94
Violent families and nonviolent neighbors, a comparison, 131-132
Vocabulary of motives, 117
"Volcanic" violence, 74-77, 80, 90
Vulnerable self concept, 157, 165-167

Wife beating, 15, 28, 89, 111-112, 115, 121, 143-144
Wife to husband violence, incidence of, 52
Woman's movement, 14, 15 ·
Working class families and physical abuse, 50

## ABOUT THE AUTHOR

RICHARD J. GELLES is an Associate Professor of Sociology at the University of Rhode Island. He has published extensively on the topics of child abuse, wife abuse, and family violence. He has appeared on numerous radio and television programs including the CBS Morning News, the CBS Evening News, the David Susskind Show, and the NBC special "Violence in America." He is currently completing a national study of intrafamily violence and is authoring a book with Murray A. Straus and Suzanne K. Steinmetz entitled, *Violence in the American Family*.